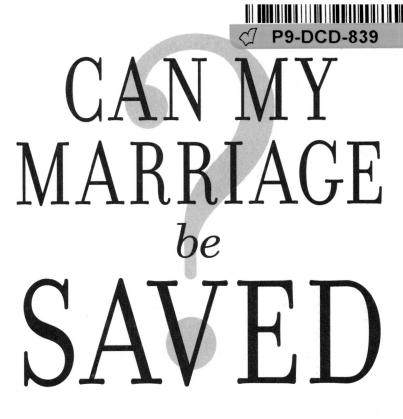

CAN MY MARRIAGE *be* SAVED

TRUE STORIES OF SAVED MARRIAGES

MAE CHAMBERS   ERIKA CHAMBERS

Pass it On
PUBLICATIONS

savedmarriagenetwork.com

PUBLICATIONS

Published by Pass It On Publications, LLC
394 W. Main Street B-11
Hendersonville, TN 37075
www.passitonpublications.com

CAN MY MARRIAGE BE SAVED? TRUE STORIES OF SAVED MARRIAGES
©2008 by Pass It On Publications LLC

Can My Marriage Be Saved? is available through most bookstores. For more information on this book and other marriage-saving resources, visit SavedMarriageNetwork.com

The web site addresses, organizations and books recommended throughout this book are offered as resources to you. These resources are not intended to imply an endorsement on the part of Pass It On Publications, nor do we vouch for their content.

First printing 2008

Edited by Erika Chambers, Jeff Gerke and Debbie Moss
Cover design by Kirk DouPonce, DogEared Design
Interior design by Patricia Reinheimer

Publisher's Cataloging-In-Publication Data
(Prepared by The Donohue Group, Inc.)

Chambers, Mae.
  Can my marriage be saved? : true stories of saved marriages / Mae Chambers, Erika Chambers.

  p. ; cm.

  Includes bibliographical references and index.
  ISBN: 978-0-9814747-0-0

1. Marriage--United States--Case studies. 2. Marital conflict--United States--Case studies. 3. Married people--United States--Psychology--Case studies. I. Chambers, Erika, 1981- II. Title.

HQ536 .C436 2008
306.872/0973

ISBN 978-0-9814747-0-0

All Scripture quotations, unless otherwise noted, are taken form the *Holy Bible New International Version NIV.* ©1973, 1978, 1984 by International Bible Society. Used by permission of Zondervan.

This book is dedicated to my parents,
Merritt and Lorraine Fogwell.

Your steadfast marriage commitment encouraged me to hold
on to hope for my own marriage when all seemed hopeless.
Without your loving example of a Covenant Marriage,
this book would never have been written.

And to John, my best friend and lifelong partner,
who lovingly reminds me every day that
ours is a marriage worth saving.

Love,
Mae

CONTENTS

FOREWORD

By Phillip H. Waugh
Executive Director, Covenant Marriage Movement

With great joy I introduce to you *Can My Marriage Be Saved?*, a book filled with true stories of God's covenant love for His people and of their surrender to His will. These stories are real-life accounts of married couples who, in times of great difficulty, struggled with their very desire to keep going. But the stories do not end there. In each case, first one and eventually both spouses come to understand that love is more than an emotion. The lives of these couples reflect what it means to be in covenant with one's spouse and with God.

Many people today view marriage merely as a legal contract. Contracts are based on rights and responsibilities and are motivated by self-centeredness rather than unconditional love. But a covenant is more than a contract. In the Bible, a covenant is an eternal promise between God and His people. The value of a "covenant marriage relationship," as opposed to a "contractual marriage agreement," lies in a person's understanding and acceptance of God's intent for marriage.

A covenant marriage is intended by God to be a lifelong relationship exemplifying unconditional love, reconciliation, sexual purity, and growth. God is always the giver of a covenant. We are the recipients. We must choose to accept and remain obedient to the covenant God has established. The foundation for such a covenant is unconditional love. A covenant relationship with a spouse should reflect God's unconditional love for His people. In actuality, a covenant relationship with a spouse is only possible through God's love.

The Covenant Marriage Movement, of which I am honored to be executive director, is a collaborative effort of more than seventy-five ministries and organizations that have united for the express purpose of joining God in what He is doing to strengthen marriages in our nation and around the world. We count among our movement some of the leading national organizations that are already impacting marriages, such as Focus on the Family, Moody Bible Institute, Promise Keepers, LifeWay Christian Resources, NAME (National Association of Marriage Enhancement), and the American Association of Christian Counselors.

The stated mission of the Covenant Marriage Movement is to restore churches and society to an understanding and practice of marriage as a covenant by applying the timeless principles of God's Word.

The challenge is for every couple in America to examine their definition of marriage with the understanding that it must be more than a contract or even a commitment. It must be a covenant.

I invite you now to read *Can My Marriage Be Saved?* and begin to glimpse the reality of God's hope for the struggling marriage in your life.

To learn more about this movement, please visit
www.covenantmarriage.com.
Phillip H. Waugh
Executive Director
Covenant Marriage Movement, Inc.

INTRODUCTION

A Note From Mae Chambers: Saved Marriage Since 1985

C hances are, you are holding this book because either *you* are in a troubled marriage or you know *someone* who is. Either way, you are desperately seeking hope for that marriage.

My name is Mae Chambers, and I have been in both positions.

In 1984 my marriage was deemed hopeless by my husband, my in-laws, all of my friends, and by three Christian counselors. Only my parents refused to join the chorus of negativity, simply stating that they loved us both and would pray for us. At that time I didn't know of *one* couple whose marriage had survived the kind of damage ours had suffered. Nevertheless, I refused to give up on my marriage. I cried out to God for hope.

In the pages that follow, you will read how God miraculously intervened to save my marriage. Soon after my husband and I reconciled, we found ourselves surrounded by other couples in marital crisis. Suddenly we were in search of hope for marriages that were crumbling all around us. My husband, John, and I were amazed at how the honest recounting of our saved marriage story inspired hope in those struggling couples, many of whom eventually reconciled.

The idea for this book came out of that experience. Our reasoning is this: if *one* saved marriage story, shared face-to-face, brought hope to dozens of couples, surely *multiple* stories, published in a nationally distributed book, could bring hope to thousands.

In this book we have compiled, from national ministries, true stories of saved marriages to offer hope to couples in crisis. At the end of each story, we list the contact information and available resources provided by the ministry associated with that story.

If you are in a troubled marriage, I encourage you to read these stories with an open mind. Ask God to show you His truth in your situation. If a particular story speaks to you, I encourage you to contact the corresponding ministry for help and encouragement.

When I believed my marriage was over, I asked God for *hope*. But He first gave me *truth*. He showed me that I was not altogether innocent. He showed me how my disrespectful, unloving attitudes had contributed to the breakdown of my marriage. Only when I acknowledged *my* part of the problem could I see His hope for change.

At some point in every saved marriage story there is a divine *aha!* moment for each partner. Divine truth precedes hope. I pray that you will find both in the following stories.

The first story is mine.

MAE *and* JOHN 1

"Once he's made up his mind for divorce, there's nothing you can do."

I simply couldn't accept the counselor's conclusion. I began to pray for God to send someone who would counsel me, not out of pity, but from the truth of God's Word.

The back door slammed at John's angry exit. The vibration jarred my dusty guitar from its lonely corner of our family room. As I reached for the fallen guitar, my mind raced back over seven years and two thousand miles to a sweltering 1977 mid-August afternoon in downtown Dayton, Ohio.

A MATCH MADE IN A MUSIC STORE

I had entered Bernie's Music Center that day in search of a new guitar, one that wouldn't hurt my fingers when I played. I had walked out two hours later, having left not only a deposit on an instrument but also an impression on the handsome young salesman, who had hurriedly copied my phone number from the layaway ticket. I learned months later that John's co-workers had promptly dubbed me "John's layaway girl."

John called me that evening. He wanted to go out with me, but I happened to have other plans. He called me every evening for the next week, but I truly happened to have previous plans every time he asked to see me. The next week John called again, this time inviting me to his apartment. Our first date consisted of sitting in his kitchen with him singing and playing his guitar and me singing harmonies to most of the songs he knew. We had instant chemistry — in more than just a sexual way, which (I later learned) was unusual for John.

That night I mentioned that I was looking for a guitarist to accompany me at a friend's November wedding. John immediately offered to play. Now we had a nice excuse to get together again — we had to practice. One practice led to another. Soon we were spending every day together and every night rehearsing. Our voices blended beautifully, and so, it seemed, did our lives.

John and I sang together at my friend's Thanksgiving wedding. John played my new guitar, which he'd redeemed from layaway just the week before. I caught the bouquet at the reception, and before the weekend was over John had asked me to marry him.

I *had* fallen in love with him — with one reservation. I considered myself a Christian, but John didn't share my faith in Christ. When he proposed, I gave a tentative yes, and then I asked John to pray for God's blessing on our engagement. John hesitated and then began to sob, saying he felt so good about me but so bad about himself.

The next morning was a Sunday, and for the first time John asked to come to church with me. The minute the pastor gave the altar call, John grabbed my hand and practically dragged me down the aisle. In one long, excited breath, John told the pastor that he wanted to become a Christian and that he wanted him to marry us as soon as possible.

I was ecstatic. Now I could marry John without reservation. As we left the church that brisk November morning we stepped out upon a pure, white blanket of freshly fallen snow.

John and I set our wedding date for the following March. We became regular churchgoers and were involved in the choir and special music programs. John was the star pupil in the "new beginners" class.

WARNING SIGNS

But not everything had become "new" in John's life. Some nights John would come over to my apartment well after midnight, stone drunk. There were angry outbursts, and he would curse and throw things.

One afternoon just days before the wedding, I discovered a stack of pornography in the back of John's closet. In tears, I carefully wrote the following words on the back of our wedding invitation: "John, I'll never be able to measure up to the women in these magazines. It hurts me to think I'm not enough for you. Love, Mae." I slipped the invitation just inside the cover of the top magazine and shoved the stack back into the darkness.

Despite my concerns, I was still in love, believing that "love believes the best." Our wedding plans continued, and John and I prerecorded our own music for the ceremony. Once again our voices blended with the smooth, mellow sounds of my layaway guitar.

We were married on a dreary day in March. Our wedding was well attended by friends, family, and church members.

Four months into our lives together, we moved to Phoenix. I was anxious to put distance between us and John's history of sex, drugs, and rock 'n' roll. John was up for the adventure of starting a new life in an unfamiliar place, a place so starkly different from the lush green landscape we had known as children.

We found our church the first Sunday we were in town. John had a job waiting for him, and two weeks later I landed a job at the local newspaper. We quickly made friends at work and in the "newly married" class at church. Although we were both working, life seemed a perpetual vacation. We continued making our music together, singing specials in church and at the occasional party.

Life was easy, money was more than enough, and we seemed

the perfect couple. We dreamed of bigger things. John put together a TV pilot. He was talented and funny, a natural entertainer. Together we designed a novelty product to sell. The Pet Rock had made someone a millionaire in the early seventies. We introduced the Punk Rock, the new cool pet for the eighties. We got some media coverage, but our creative ideas still weren't profitable. Never mind that; we were having fun.

We decided to add to the fun by starting a family. Erika was born three years into our marriage, precisely on her due date, and she continued to be the most accommodating child. We were now the perfect couple with the perfect child. She was bright and perceptive, and I, having a teaching degree, was determined to give her the best education at the earliest age. One afternoon, when one-year-old Erika burst into tears at the sight of more early reading flashcards, I knew I'd pushed too hard.

I began to petition my husband for another child. "We need a second child to help take the pressure off of Erika," I reasoned. A new baby would bring balance to our little family.

DISCONNECTING

Erika had been such a good baby, and I'd longed to stay home with her. But with that first new baby came the new house, the new minivan, and the newly acquired debt. I couldn't afford not to work, so I arranged for day care in a private home and returned to my job in newspaper advertising. But good infant care was hard to find, and after five failed childcare arrangements in Erika's first year, I began to dream of starting my own childcare referral service, a business I could run from home.

John had been in strong opposition to my quitting a well-paying job to start a home business. But I was so distraught over my daughter's unstable day-care situation that I made the move despite his objections. Then, to prove to John that my new home business could be successful, I threw myself into building my childcare referral service, The Infant Tree, from our living room. I would be on the phone early in the morning making last-minute childcare arrangements for a sick caregiver or at dinnertime calling a potential client for an appointment the next day.

Now that I was working from home, we could have that second child we had discussed. Life was fulfilling for me. Erika was doing well in a Montessori preschool, my business was bringing in enough for us to get by, and I was expecting our second child.

But amidst all my happiness, I was too busy to notice that life was not fulfilling for John. I was so consumed with passion for my business and my children that I, as John later put it, relegated him to the back burner with the heat turned off. He got involved again with alcohol and drugs, and his verbal abuse climbed to an all-time high.

In retrospect, it shouldn't have surprised me when, three months before our second daughter was born, John stood before me in our kitchen and declared that he no longer loved me but would stick around for the sake of the baby.

In despair I threw myself on the cold, hard floor, cursing myself for being so unlovable.

Seven months later, when Alyson was four months and Erika three years old, John announced he was divorcing me. It was Thanksgiving weekend, seven years after we had so joyfully announced our engagement. There was no pure, white blanket of snow. We were wandering in a desert, lost and wounded.

●   ●   ●

The slamming of the back door had woken little Alyson from her nap. Her squeals jolted me back into the present moment. With a deep sigh, I cradled my treasured classical guitar for just a moment before going to get the baby. It was then that I noticed the fracture—a break in the neck of my layaway guitar, just above the body. My hot tears splashed down upon the dusty frets.

Of course, my cherished guitar is broken, I thought wryly. *Broken and neglected, just like my marriage.*

Baby Alyson squealed again. Gingerly, I placed my fractured guitar in its velvet-lined case and stood it back in its lonely corner. I quickly dressed the baby and rushed out to get Erika from preschool. I had an appointment with another counselor that day.

This would be the fourth time I had sought advice on my disintegrating marriage. The first three counselors, after hearing of John's re-involvement with drugs and alcohol, his raging verbal abuse, and his adamant refusal to seek help, all advised me to go along with the divorce. Sympathetic, they referred me to their divorce recovery classes. "It takes *two* to work on a marriage," they said. "Unfortunately, once he's made up his mind for divorce, there's nothing *you* can do."

But I simply couldn't accept their conclusion. I began to pray for God to send someone who would counsel me not out of pity but from the truth of God's Word.

And so I found myself in yet another counselor's office, hoping to find that person. Once again I told my sad story of a failing marriage, this time to Trish. She too was sympathetic to my situation. But instead of dismissing me to a divorce recovery class, she challenged me to go home, get alone with God, and honestly ask Him to show me what *I* had done to cause problems in my marriage. My face flushed with anger, but I held my tongue. Obviously she had missed the fact that I was a *victim* in this mess of a marriage. *John* was the guilty one.

I was furious at her suggestion, yet I was desperate enough to take her advice. As I mumbled a feeble prayer asking God to examine my heart, He began to play back the tapes in my mind. The next several days were filled with flashbacks—images and conversations spanning my seven years with John. This behind-the-scenes footage exposed my disrespectful and inconsiderate attitudes toward my husband. I cried for a week, and the bitterness I'd held toward John began to ebb away as I realized I was *not* innocent.

I visited with Trish a second time, recounting God's response to my prayer. Trish referred me to a local "Standers" group, a weekly gathering of married people whose spouses had left them, either emotionally or physically. I was quick to stand with them, eager to learn how to show God's unconditional love to my husband. God had rekindled hope for my marriage. Those first three counselors were wrong, I thought triumphantly. There *was* something I could do.

I could allow God to change *me*.

John, however, was not impressed with my breakthrough. He rejected my apologies. When I assured him I still loved him, he shot back that he certainly did *not* love me and never had. "You can't change," he said flatly, "any more than a tiger can change its stripes."

This was going to be harder than I had thought. But I was more determined than ever to show John unconditional love, despite his resistance. When John shouted insults, I tried to return a soft answer. I looked for opportunities to show him respect and honor, and I praised him whenever it was appropriate to do so. I stopped nagging about his drinking and "late nights at the office." I resolved to stop speaking negatively about him to others, and instead, I enlisted the prayer support of a few trusted friends and family members.

Nine months passed, with little change in our relationship. Unwilling to even talk about our marriage, John continued to threaten divorce; he had long since removed his wedding band. He was still living in our house, as he had saved no money for divorce expenses, but he made it clear to me and everyone else that we were no longer a couple.

Late one night, I found him on the phone in our family room, whispering softly to a woman on the other end. I insisted he move out the next day. As I helped him pack his things, I told him again that I loved him and believed our marriage could be saved. However, I could no longer subject the children and myself to his destructive behaviors.

John was excited about his newfound independence. I too relished my freedom from the constant anger and verbal abuse from a tortured soul bent on self-destruction. Preparing for an extended time of separation, I put the house up for sale. I had no doubt that God would provide for me and my little girls. But I implored my prayer partners to join me in intense prayer on John's behalf.

Early on a Saturday morning two weeks into the separation, I received an unexpected phone call from John. I was taken aback by his entreating voice, so different from the cynical, bitter tone I'd heard on the phone just the night before. Softly, earnestly, he asked to come home. I invited him to come over, to stand before me and relate what dramatic event could have changed his mind overnight. This is his story.

In John's Words . . .

It was nearly seven years into our marriage. Mae and I had grown apart. Our true selves were beginning to shine through. She was the oldest of three from a "boring," Christian, white-bread-and-mayonnaise, Hoosier family, in which getting home from church in time to see Sunday night's episode of *Bonanza* was the high point of the week.

I, on the other hand, was the "sensitive and artistic" middle son of three boys, raised in an upper-middle-class family. Mom stayed home while Dad worked and played hard and fast as a professional engineer. At age thirteen I learned to make a perfect Bloody Mary and, without missing a beat, could light party guests' cigarettes with one hand, thanks to my trusty Zippo.

By age fifteen I was making money playing bass guitar and singing in local bands. By age twenty-two I had a college degree in TV production but chose to play music in a 1950s' style bar band known as Vasoline Alley. At age twenty-five, with half my hearing severely dulled, I left the spotlight to sell guitars, amps, and microphones to working musicians and wannabes. I still pursued the rock 'n' roll lifestyle, though. I had a two-room apartment where friends would come to drink, smoke dope, and look through my collection of pornographic magazines. After a lifetime of sharing homes, dorms, and hotel rooms with brothers, roommates, and band members, I finally had my own place.

Then *she* walked in.

August 1977: I was her salesman, but she did the closing.

My dad used to say, "Why make one woman miserable when you can make them all happy?" Well, that philosophy just flew out the window. Dad also warned, "John, be careful. If you chase a girl long enough, she'll catch you!" As it turned out, he was right.

Fast forward to 1984. I was making one woman (and myself) miserable. It was mutually decided that I should move out. Every day had become a collision of two worlds. At home I had become irrelevant. At work I was a successful corporate video writer-shooter-editor. I went to work each day convinced that I was God's gift to women, and the attention I received from my female co-workers confirmed that notion in my mind. This was attention I wasn't getting at home.

Apparently, dysfunction was in my DNA. My dad was then on his second wife. My mom had become bitter and alone with nothing left to nurse but a bottle. My younger brother was on number two of three wives. My older brother's wife was about to divorce and abandon him for a lesbian lover. In the end, pride, lust, intoxication, and rage were the only things my family shared.

It only made sense, then, for my marriage to fail as well. Mae had her business and the girls. I had my work, other women, and plenty of money for spiced rum and Coke—and the other kind of "coke." The Christian thing was a distant memory. After all, I had really only "accepted Christ" so Mae would marry me. It was time to be who I really was.

Mae was beginning to reveal her inherited genetics as well. Her parents were quiet Christians living out their functional marriage, which to me, seemed boring and predictable. Divorce, for them, was not an option. It all made sense to me, since I believed people like that didn't have enough passion to fight about anything. No spice, no excitement, always accepting and even-keeled.

And now Mae was beginning to act more like them. For months Mae hadn't been the nag I had grown to hate. Instead, she had become pleasant and unshaken—regardless of the emotional projectiles I threw in her direction. This repelled me even more—at first.

Then came my move to "Hell House."

Although I was an asthmatic with allergies to dust, mold, mildew, and pet dander, I moved in with George, a chain-smoking, recently divorced friend who owned four cats. George needed help with the rent, and I needed a base from which to pursue my passions with no accountability, despite the fact that living there left me constantly sniffling, sneezing, and gasping for air.

Shortly after moving in with him, on one of those rare nights when I was sober and sleeping alone, a gentle inner voice woke me up and began to ask questions.

"John, if you continue the alcohol abuse, where will you be in five years?"

I began to mentally list the calamities that might befall me: I might die in a drunk driving accident. I might die of cirrhosis of the liver. I might lose my job and be out on the streets. My life could be destroyed.

The inner voice continued, "Who came to kill, steal, and destroy, John?"

I knew enough of the Bible to answer this question. "Satan."

"Who loves you, John?"

I knew this answer too. "God loves me."

I drifted back to sleep but was awakened again by the same voice. "John, if you continue the cocaine abuse, where will you be in five years?"

Again, I listed the possible consequences of my cocaine abuse: prison, AIDS due to eventual intravenous injections, and the obvious financial ruin.

"Who came to kill, steal, and destroy, John?"

"Satan."

"Who loves you, John?"

"God loves me."

I closed my eyes, but that persistent voice was not finished with me. "John, if you continue the adultery, where will you be in five years?"

Disease, divorce, maybe even death at the hands of an angry husband.

"Who came to kill, steal, and destroy?"

"Satan, Satan, Satan!"

"Who loves you, John?" the inner voice said tenderly.

This time I spoke it aloud. "God. God loves me!"

Then the gentle voice asked the final question of the evening. "Who else loves you, John?"

"My wife!" Even as I said the words, my answer surprised me. "My wife loves me!"

Her prayers had prevailed.

In that moment, my idea of marriage was transformed from the image of a prison to a picture of Disneyland. Both places have walls. In prison you're desperate to escape your confinement, but in Disneyland your inner child loves everything within the park's boundaries, so you beg your parents to let you stay.

I couldn't wait for morning. I couldn't wait to call my wife.

A Changed Man

When John came over and told me what had happened, I could clearly see he had experienced a genuine change of heart. Although he had ardently resisted the guidance of any human counselor, John had responded to God's Holy Spirit, the mighty Counselor.

In psychological therapy a counselor asks the right questions in the right sequence. If the patient listens to his or her own answers, they supposedly cure themselves. That night the Holy Spirit asked the right questions. John listened to his own answers. I later found out that not only was he cured, but also it was as if John's DNA code had literally been reprogrammed.

I had prayed often for God to prepare me for the moment John would decide to come home. God had set before me a step-by-step plan of reconciliation.

I began by inviting John to join me in an intensive, thirty-six-hour seminar that would give biblical instruction for every area of our lives. John agreed that we needed to build a solid foundation for our renewed life together. On the second night of the seminar, the topic was alcoholism. John was so impacted by the truth that evening that he vowed to give up his drinking. He has kept that promise to this day, more than twenty-three years later. His desire for drugs and the appeal of adultery were also dealt with that week. Those issues have never resurfaced.

In an effort to rebuild trust, John became accountable to me regarding his whereabouts. I appreciated him calling me whenever he reached his destination. This was just one of several things John began to do to rekindle our love and strengthen our commitment to one another. He began taking me on romantic dates where we would sit and talk for hours. We would talk and *laugh*. John's sense of humor was one of the first things that had attracted me to him, and I had missed laughing together. During those dates I began to notice John looking at me differently—like he had when we'd first met. We were both falling in love all over again.

A few months after John's homecoming, I remembered my broken guitar. I told John about that gloomy afternoon a year earlier when I'd discovered the crack in the special instrument that had brought us together.

"I'm sorry, honey," John said compassionately. "Let me see if I can fix that for you." He carefully removed the guitar from its case and asked me to show him the fracture.

I pointed to the base of the neck, and we both leaned in to examine the damage.

"Are you sure you didn't have someone glue this for you?" John asked. "All I can see is a hairline crack."

I felt warm all over. *Of course my cherished guitar had been restored*, I thought, smiling. *Restored and cared for. Just like my marriage.*

—*Mae and John Chambers*

❧ • ❧

Mae and John Chambers celebrated thirty years of marriage in March 2008. They currently live outside Nashville, Tennessee, with their twelve-year-old son, Adam. Their two grown daughters, Erika and Alyson, live close by. Alyson was joyfully joined in covenant marriage to Terry West in July of 2007.

John does video production for their church and co-owns a plastic gift card company with Mae. For the past twenty years, John and Mae have continually been involved in one-on-one mentoring of couples in martial crisis.

Mae Chambers and her daughter, Erika, are the founders of SavedMarriageNetwork.com, a Web site full of "marriage-saving" resources, including information about and links to national ministries and organizations specializing in crisis couple assistance and counseling.

The Saved Marriage Network
Mae Chambers
www.savedmarriagenetwork.com

CLINT *and* PENNY

*She came home late from work one Friday evening, greeted by
the blinking red light on her answering machine. She never
expected that blinking light to represent a message left in that
familiar, deep Southern voice—a voice she hadn't heard in
over a decade.*

February 18, 2002
Dear Clint,
    *I have no idea if this letter will even reach you. I pray that it will.
As a matter of fact, my intent to contact you has been bathed in prayer
for almost a year. Now that I think I finally have your latest address,
there's no excuse for me to hesitate any longer, except for my own fears as
to how you might react or that you will not respond. Honestly, I don't
really expect anything in return from you, unless you feel led to do so. My
hope is that I would at least know that you received this and read it.*

Penny had put off writing this letter for as long as she possibly
could. After spending years running from the pain of her past, and
nearly losing her faith in the process, God was gently drawing her
back and healing her heart. And as she grew closer to God, she felt
strongly that it was time to reconcile the broken relationships she
had left behind so long ago.

As she set out to make amends with former friends and col-
leagues, there was one person she could not bring herself to contact,
one relationship she had walked away from more than ten years

prior. "God, please don't make me revisit that!" But the time had come, and she knew it. So she sat down and poured her heart onto the page.

> *My intent in writing this is to bring healing to my life and hope-fully yours. It is not to bring you pain or open old wounds. As I've been actively seeking the Lord's will for my life over the last three years, one thing has been clear. He has shown me ways in which I clearly left my relationship with you unresolved. He has shown me that I made some serious mistakes with huge consequences. He has directed me to apolo-gize to you and ask your forgiveness.*

LOOKING BACK

Penny and Clint first met on a baseball field. That was fitting, since they both shared a love for sports. Penny was immediately taken by Clint's chiseled good looks, luscious Southern drawl, and obvi-ous passion for God and people. Clint was captivated by Penny's vivacious personality as well as her impressive self-discipline and strong desire to serve the Lord.

However, much of their mutual attraction was due to the fact that they were both fighters. Each had acquired several battle scars through their lives, scars they had both carefully patched over with a strong facade of self-reliance.

Penny had endured a tumultuous childhood, which taught her to keep her chin up and her eyes dry. As a result, she never actually learned how to process the pain she had experienced during those early years. Then, as a young woman, Penny was swept into a dis-turbingly inappropriate relationship with a pastor, which left her heavy with feelings of shame and unworthiness—and a mistrust of men.

Clint had experienced his share of life's blows as well. He had survived the early death of his father, two tours in Vietnam, and two failed marriages. Although Clint and Penny had openly shared their painful experiences with God and each other, they both still carried more baggage than they realized.

After a whirlwind engagement, full of romance and adventure, their church family gave them the wedding of their dreams, and the couple energetically began life's journey together. They threw themselves into church leadership and activities. After nearly a year of wedded bliss, they signed up for a two-week mission trip to Haiti. Even with several months of training prior to the trip, nothing could have prepared them for what they were about to experience.

What they expected to be a positive spiritual experience quickly turned into a traumatic one, particularly for Penny. She had a hard time understanding the extreme poverty and desperation that surrounded her. She was shaken to her core and found herself questioning the God she thought she knew so well.

After that mission trip their marriage was never the same. Compounded by the bulk of overcommitted service to their church, their careers, Penny's disillusioning role as a stepmother to Clint's young son, and trials within both of their extended families, their snow-white facade began to crack, curl, and peel. It was as if every disappointment in Penny's childhood and young adult life had converged at this point. Coupled with the mounting pressure she placed on herself to be the perfect wife and stepmother, it was all becoming more weight than she could bear.

During this time, Penny became increasingly involved in a relationship with a student she met in college. What began as an innocent friendship soon developed into something much deeper. While she resisted her friend's unwanted sexual advances at first, she gradually let down her guard and was quickly engaged in a full-blown affair. Less than two years after she walked down the aisle, she walked out on her marriage.

Nothing could fill the void in her heart—not her dutiful service to God, not her promising career, not even her husband. Living in a world where she felt ineffective as a wife and ill-equipped as a stepmother, her sadness consumed her. Unable to cope any longer, she left her family and her faith behind her and did not look back for a very, very long time.

> *I have been on my own for several years now. Solitude has drawn me to a relationship with Christ that I never thought possible. I am continually amazed by His grace and unconditional love for me, despite my many mistakes. . . . It's hard to believe how much time has passed and how far apart we are. It is my hope and prayer that this letter might begin to bridge the gap between us and that God will soften your heart to consider my words.*
>
> *Clint, please pray about this. Know that I will continue praying long after this letter leaves my hands and is placed into His . . . and ultimately, yours.*
>
> *Penny*

RECONNECTING

Once she mailed that letter to Clint, Penny left the outcome completely in God's hands. She was at peace for the first time in many years.

Until she came home late from work one Friday evening and was greeted by the blinking red light on her answering machine. She never expected that blinking light to represent a message left in that familiar, deep Southern voice—a voice she hadn't heard in over a decade.

His message said, among other things, that he had received

her letter that day and would make "one more attempt" to call at 8:00 p.m.

Penny was absolutely stunned at hearing Clint's message. She fell to her knees and sobbed in desperate prayer. Penny was not about to miss that call. After calling her best friend in utter panic, Penny sat alone with God and waited. As the minute hand struck the top of the clock, her telephone rang. Clint's first words to her, spoken in that deep, familiar drawl, were, "Is that you?"

It's me, all right, she thought, *but a very different "me" than the young woman you once knew.*

The humility and gentleness in his voice spoke of Clint's own transformation. He was a changed man, toting a tone of one who had encountered a similar level of intimacy, mercy, and forgiveness from God that she had.

Their conversation lasted five hours. By the end of it they had put everything on the table. They cried, reminisced, and even laughed together. Most importantly, they exchanged words of regret and forgiveness well into the early morning hours. As they said their good-byes, they prayed together and wished one another well. Their work was complete, and Penny never expected to hear from Clint again.

God, however, was working behind the scenes, gently drawing their hearts back together as He had so gently drawn each of them back to Himself. The day after their marathon phone call, Clint was busy writing a ten-page letter of his own, which Penny would receive just two days later.

To My Dearest Penny,

This is the longest and most honest letter that I have written since you and I were together. Last night was one of the most eventful nights of my last twelve years. I had a lot of pain and guilt in my heart because of the way you and I ended our relationship. What I am getting ready to say right now is something I never thought I would say to you . . .

Penny, if all you wanted from me is my forgiveness so you can move on with your life, you have it, and I want you to enjoy it. I want the best for you, my lady. May the Lord bless you. But I still have unconditional love for you in my heart. This is not meant to play with your emotions or with your heart . . .

Boy, this next part is hard to write, Penny. If it is your desire to meet, I say that you fly from California and I fly from Florida, and we meet somewhere in the middle and spend some time together to pray and do some healthy talking about our ministries and what we feel God wants us to finish for Him for the rest of our lives on Earth. . . . I would like to see if you and I could get it right this time.

His words turned Penny's heart upside-down, as they had so many years ago. She called him that evening, and they began to seek God's will about if, when, and how they might begin bridging the wide gap between them.

Over the next several months, God continued the healing work He had begun in each of them. They both contacted several friends and pastors, who committed to praying about their relationship. In addition, Clint and Penny shared weekly devotions over the phone. They e-mailed back and forth. And they searched the Scriptures and wrote letters to one another. They also exchanged family photographs, videos, and mementos to fill in the missing years.

For the first several weeks after they began to converse, Penny walked around in a daze, waiting for the other shoe to drop or for someone to wake her from what had to be a dream. Each day after work, she rushed home and flipped open her laptop to scan through her e-mails for a message from Clint. And each day, she was not disappointed. Eventually, she came to believe that all of this had really happened—but she printed out every one of his e-mails, just to be sure. Later, Clint told her that he had done the same thing.

Finally, on May 24, 2002, Clint and Penny came face-to-face in the terminal of Denver International Airport. While Penny was relieved to have made it all the way up the walkway without tripping in her high heels, she did indeed fall that weekend. Once again, as she had in 1987, she fell in love with Clint, and he with her.

They fit together hand-in-glove, and their reunion was seamless from beginning to end. God stitched up the gaping eleven-year hole in both their hearts with His threads of forgiveness and hope.

After their initial meeting in the terminal, they picked up their bags and their rental car. Prior to pulling out of the parking lot, they joined their hands in prayer, asking God to have His way with the remainder of their weekend and the rest of their lives.

Once they arrived at the hotel and checked into their respective rooms, they decided to part company and freshen up a bit before their date. When Clint appeared at Penny's hotel room door an hour later, trailing behind him was a medium-sized black suitcase. She had no idea as to the contents of the bag until he flung it up onto her bed and asked her to open it.

Inside were the trinkets and treasures he had saved from their wedding, all the memories she had left behind. The suitcase was stuffed full of wedding cards and photographs. In addition, the actual items from their ceremony were there, including the silver goblets from their first toast as husband and wife.

Kneeling down at the foot of the bed, Penny sobbed and sifted through the contents of the suitcase and the kaleidoscope of memories that accompanied each item. Clint told her how he had placed all of those items in a box after she left and had carried it with him as he moved from house to house — nine moves in all. When he left California for Florida, he decided to finally dump it all for good.

"I can't explain it, but something, or rather, *Someone*, stopped me from throwing it all away," he told her.

In addition to unpacking that suitcase, there were many other more figurative pieces of baggage that needed to be unloaded that weekend. With years of journals in hand, they spread out every question, sorrow, sin, and regret before one another on the grass of a park in downtown Denver.

Slowly, the missing pieces were filled in as they shared things about their childhood and adolescent years that they had never been vulnerable enough to tell one another during their marriage.

Sunday morning, as their reunion weekend was coming to a close, they held their own private worship service in Penny's hotel room. After a very emotional prayer time, before Penny even rose from her knees, Clint asked if she still had her wedding band. She reached into her bag and pulled out a brown suede pouch, which held her ring. Clint took his wedding band from a chain around his neck. Placing both rings in the palm of his hand, he closed his eyes and prayed. Lifting his eyes, he asked, "Penny, will you marry me . . . again?"

She blubbered back an emphatic, "Yes!"

On August 17, 2002, they were married once again in front of family and friends—this time, for life.

God's restoration of their shattered marriage far surpassed their expectations and the expectations of anyone else. They committed to spending the first year of their remarriage seeking God's direction as to how to make certain that this time around they put God first in their individual lives and in their marriage. They each committed to having daily quiet times with God, meeting regularly with their prayer partners, and getting plugged into a good Christian church. They also made sure they maintained honest conversations with each other and rebuilt the trust that was broken in their first marriage to one another. In addition, they agreed to take a retreat four times each year to seek God's guidance for their future and to continue the healing work He had started in their relationship.

As time passed and the word began to spread about Clint and Penny's miraculous reconciliation, churches began asking them to come and share their story. Each time they told others about what God had done in their marriage, they sensed Him drawing them toward a ministry to help couples in crisis. However, they wanted to be absolutely certain that this was God's desire and that they weren't running ahead of Him with their own agenda.

Several years after they reconciled, they formed Inverse Ministries, a nonprofit ministry of reconciliation that supports couples in crisis. Through the work of Inverse Ministries, Clint and Penny now serve God as full-time "marriage missionaries," traveling across the nation and sharing their story in churches and homes to everyone God brings across their path. God continually uses Clint and Penny's story in a uniquely personal way to encourage even the most hopeless couples. Having been divorced for over a decade, they know a thing or two about "hopeless" situations.

When Penny sat down to write that letter to Clint in 2002, she never imagined an outcome like this. But now she and Clint know that not only is God the Redeemer, but He is also the ultimate Romancer. And they are humbled daily by the knowledge that theirs is a very special chapter in the greatest love story of all time.

— *Erika Chambers (with Penny Bragg)*

Source: Penny A. Bragg, *The Path of Most Resistance—A True Story of Reconciliation and Hope* (Dublin, CA, Clint and Penny Bragg, 2004)

෬•෬

Clint and Penny Bragg are the founders and directors of Inverse Ministries. These "marriage missionaries" travel nationwide providing a ministry of reconciliation during their forty-day marriage mission trips. Each of these forty-day mission trips, focused on a particular region of the country, is an opportunity to share their own remarkable story and equip couples with practical tools for strengthening their relationships with each other and God.

Clint and Penny also teach marriage ministry leaders and pastors how to implement effective, ongoing support to couples in marital crisis. Available seminars include "Building Resilient Relationships: Tangible Tools to Support Couples in Crisis"; "Discovering God's Vision for Your Marriage" (for couples or small group leaders); and "Foundations for a Ministry of Reconciliation in Your Church."

Inverse Ministries, Inc.
Clint and Penny Bragg
1648 Taylor Rd., #607
Port Orange, FL 32128
www.inverseministries.org
reconcile@inverseministries.org

GARY *and* MONA   3

"God, I need a miracle here. We're sitting here breathing, though I know we're dying. But I don't know why I have to die when the sin is not mine! I didn't do this. Gary did this. She did this. I know I wasn't a perfect wife, but who is?"

GARY

It must have been about 9:30 as I pulled into the driveway. Everything looked dark and settled down for the evening. As I stopped the car, my heart pounded in my chest like never before. For a moment, I wondered if I might be having a heart attack. I took a deep breath, got out of the car, and walked in the back door of the house. The boys were in bed. The house was quiet as I made my way to our bedroom.

Our bedroom.

I wondered if that would still be true in the aftermath of the bomb I was about to drop. Should I really go through with this? This could be the end of everything I had known as my life: my family, my church, my business, and my friends. Every area of my life would be affected by the event about to occur. Should I tell her, or should I just keep living the lie?

I had spent the past two hours in my pastor's office confessing my sin. At first, he thought I was joking. He never imagined I had the capacity to do such a thing and keep it hidden for so long. Finally, as tears streamed down my face, he knew I was gravely

35

serious. He was saying great words of spiritual wisdom and encouragement, but his shock and disbelief were still apparent.

He asked if Mona knew. I shook my head. He looked me in the eye. "Do you intend to tell her?"

I nodded. "I need to go now and tell her."

Now I was home, and I knew what I had to do. I walked into the bedroom. The lamp on her bedside table glowed. There she lay, reading a book.

She looked up. "How was your meeting"? Then our eyes met. A look of concern appeared on her face. "Honey, what's wrong?"

I hadn't rehearsed anything. I had no words. I just sat down on the bed and looked at her.

"You're scaring me," she said.

I started to cry.

"Now you're really scaring me."

Finally I managed to whisper. "I've betrayed you."

Her eyes seemed to stare through me. "What?"

"I've been unfaithful to you."

Her stare went from distant to direct and cold. "With whom?"

I said the name. It was one of Mona's best friends.

"I knew it," she said. But I knew she hadn't known. Now she was shell-shocked. "How long?"

I whispered, "A long time."

"*How long?*"

"A couple of years."

"*Years?* Ever since you started working with her?"

"Almost."

Her lip quivered.

As her world crumbled around her feet, my heart raced again. There was more. I hadn't told her everything. There had also been a one-night stand with another woman. Should I tell her? Might as well get it all out now. When I confessed that part, I honestly thought she was going to pass out.

After a long, eerie silence she said, "We need to talk. But not here."

The boys were old enough to be left alone, so we got in the car and drove. We didn't speak a word on that drive to the office where we both worked. Once we settled in the conference room, the flurry of questions began.

"Do you love her?"

"No, I love you."

"Do you want a divorce?"

"No, I want to stay with you. Do *you* want a divorce?"

"I don't know what I want. Why did you do this?"

I didn't know how to answer that question. I honestly didn't know how I had gotten where I was. I explained that it was a friendship that had gotten out of control and that I had felt trapped. I had never stopped loving Mona. Soon she began to ask questions about the one-night stand. I tried to explain, but knew I could not justify my actions. I shut my mouth and began to cry again.

There seemed to be nothing left to say that night, so we went home. I offered to sleep on the couch, but Mona declined my offer. As we lay beside one another in our bed, everything was quiet and still — but I knew the explosion was yet to come. I was sure her mind was whirling with thoughts, bouncing from one horrific scenario to another. All I could do was lie next to her and watch as her entire foundation cracked and fell away. Every now and then a tear would roll down her cheek and a sob would escape her throat.

My God, what have I done? One thing was certain: we would never be the same again. *God, please forgive me.*

MONA

On the night Gary told me about his affair, my life divided into three categories: before, during, and after the affair. I didn't know which time period was worst.

Before was a sham, a fraud I had perpetuated. I had believed I had a good marriage and a great husband, but had he ever really loved me? *During* was nothing but being lied to and being so very stupid. How many times and in how many ways had I commented to my "friend" about what a good marriage we had—and all the while, she was sleeping with my husband! *After* was hell, plain and simple. Pain every day, all day. I was incapable of being a good mother, a good friend, or a good employee. Pain seemed to be the only thing that wasn't a lie. But how much longer would the pain go on? How much more could our family take?

Gary and I entered counseling, which helped, but it still took so much energy to act like a normal human being. Performing the everyday activities of a woman and mother required reaching into the deep recesses of myself and dragging up whatever little bit of strength and fortitude I could find. By the time dinner and dishes were done, homework completed, and the kids settled into their rooms for the night, I was exhausted. During those days, it took everything I had just to breathe. This "healing process" had gone on longer than I had expected. But I couldn't pretend to be healed if I wasn't. I knew Gary was ready to be done with it. Too bad! This was his doing.

I did have to give Gary credit, though. He was repentant. He made himself an open book and gave me permission to ask any question I needed to. He answered a lot of questions I know he didn't want to.

GARY

I don't know how to describe Mona during those days. She was consumed with pain and questions. I lost count of how many times she asked the same questions. And I was getting mad. I knew I didn't have any right to get mad. It was my fault we were here in the first place. But it's hard to answer a question that you know is going to blow your wife's world apart. Here you are trying to rebuild the marriage, and yet with your complete honesty you seem to be causing more pain.

I did have to agree that she had the right to determine what she did and did not want to hear, though. I hadn't asked her permission before bringing this sin into our home. If she was going to live with the consequences of it, then she had the right to determine what she needed to know. If we had any chance of rebuilding this marriage, there was no more room for lies or half-truths.

MONA

I remember praying, *God, I need a miracle here. We're sitting here breathing, though I know we're dying. But I don't know why I have to die when the sin is not mine! I didn't do this. Gary did this. She did this. I know I wasn't a perfect wife, but who is?*

My mind was racing, and the conversations—both in my head and in the counselor's office that day—were not going as I wanted. We were discussing everything *but* the adultery. I remembered that in an earlier session the counselor had suggested I read a book on codependency. I had almost laughed out loud. My faults lay in the area of control, not the pitiful "How can I please my man?" mentality. I remember looking at him and saying, "You think *I'm* codependent?"

He looked at me calmly. "I know you are."

I went ahead and took the book home, but just to prove him wrong. I read it, and before long I realized he was probably right. I hadn't realized people like me could be called "codependent." I always thought codependent people were the ones being controlled, not the ones doing the controlling.

Today the counselor grabbed another book. Only this time it was a Bible. How could I object to this one? I claimed to be a Christian. I claimed to love this Book. But I already knew what God said about adultery. He opened it and read Ephesians 4:31–32.

> Get rid of all bitterness, rage and anger, brawling and slander, along with every form of malice. Be kind and compassionate to one another, forgiving each other, just as in Christ God forgave you.

Wait a minute. This wasn't about adultery. It wasn't even about marriage. We were going to get a lesson on *forgiveness*? Didn't this guy understand the wound of adultery? He pulled out a pad of paper and wrote down these words: "bitterness," "rage," "anger," "brawling," "slander," and "malice." He proceeded to define them.

Did I really need this? True, I saw myself way too clearly in what he was saying, but didn't I have a *right* to these emotions? Look what had been done to me! He then drew two stick figures and wrote the words "critical spirit" between them. He agreed that only God could meet all the needs of another person, yet He instructed us in the Bible on how to treat one another. The counselor went on to define kindness, compassion, and a *forgiving* spirit.

The conviction of that drawing and those definitions were overwhelming. I could barely speak. I wasn't a shrew, but I did have a critical spirit. It slipped out sometimes. More importantly, I knew that Gary had experienced my critical spirit much too often. He said he didn't think he was even important to me anymore. How could he think that? *God, please tell me this affair didn't happen because of how I've treated him.*

I was just tired. I had three active little boys. I had a stressful job. Somewhere along the line, I had run out of resources, desire, kindness, and compassion for my husband. I had figured Gary loved me enough and knew me well enough to understand that our time would come later. What was that adage? "Life is what happens while you're making other plans."

The counselor's words broke through to me then. "There will never be a good enough reason for what Gary chose to do." He explained that Gary's adultery was his way of dealing with our problems. But, he said, if we really wanted to heal, we would both need to identify those problems and deal with them together in a healthy way.

GARY

"Where is the anger?"

I looked at my Christian counselor, his head cocked to one side, his forehead crinkled, and a very determined, pondering look on his face as he repeated himself. "Where is the anger?"

This was one of my first sessions alone with him. I had just spilled my guts. "How could I have done this to such a perfect wife? How could I have been so selfish?"

But he just kept staring at me. "Where is the anger?"

I didn't know what he was talking about. *I* was the bad guy here. *I* was the black-hearted liar, the adulterer! I didn't have any right to be angry. I asked him what he meant.

He smiled. "I just don't see the anger here. I know it's there. Nobody does what you did without it. You must be angry about something Mona did or didn't do. You aren't being honest with yourself if you deny that she had anything to do with all this."

"Wait a minute!" I said. "This isn't her fault. *I'm* the one who had the affair."

"Yes, you did," he said. "But a relationship is a two-sided thing. If you really want to heal your marriage, you're going to have to move beyond blaming yourself and start looking at your relationship honestly from top to bottom."

He told me to go home and do some soul-searching. He wanted me to get alone with God and ask Him to reveal to my heart the absolute truth about my relationship with Mona. And so I did.

As I prayed, I kept thinking back to a time when Mona and I were in the kitchen. The dogs and the kids were underfoot as usual, and the decibel level was a little high, but I had just learned to live with it. I remember coming up behind Mona while she was stirring the spaghetti sauce on the stove. As I placed my hands on her hips, I felt her stiffen and pull away. I leaned over to give her a kiss, and she gave me a stiff-necked "grandma" peck on the lips. "Our time will come later," she said.

I understood what she meant. She was saying that once the kids were grown, once all the important jobs were done, once everything in life that had real meaning was taken care of, then and *only* then would there be time for us, for me. That night I asked myself how I had fallen so low on her priority list. Then I just filed the thought away.

But now, the more I thought about it, the more I realized what had been lying under the surface of my mind. Mona had time for everyone else—the kids, family, friends, church, work, Bible study, and even her social life. Everyone and everything but me!

Wait just a minute. If I had really been bothered that much, why hadn't I just gone to Mona, sat her down, and had a heart-to-heart? I knew the answer to that question. I am the epitome of a conflict-avoider. And at that low point in our relationship, I would have done anything to avoid conflict.

MONA

More than a year after Gary's confession, I was still looking for answers. I heard my voice asking the same questions, heard Gary answering the same questions—again. It was almost as if I were off in a corner, watching two people on a path they didn't want to be on, yet having no idea how to get off. I knew the answer before he said it.

I searched for a way to elicit new information, trying to figure out what I needed to know now. And then a thought crossed my mind: *I don't care.* But it wasn't, "I don't care because there's nothing left in me to care with." This was, "I just plain don't care to know any more," because I'd heard it all before. I took a quick emotional inventory. Pain? Slight, but not consuming. Sadness? Not really. Tears? Gone. This was weird. Inside me was something I hadn't felt in such a long time. Disinterest. I simply wasn't interested in the details of the affair anymore.

Oh, my precious Lord! What did this mean? I couldn't imagine I would ever feel this way. Would it last? I didn't care. I was finally ready to move forward. So I interrupted my husband in mid-answer. "Gary, could we talk about something else?"

GARY AND MONA

At the beginning of our recovery process we were desperate to find another couple to encourage us, another couple to just sit across from us and say we could make it through this very dark and terrifying time. We wanted them to tell us that *we* could make it because *they* had made it and now have a marriage worth saving.

But there was no one. Our counselor could not find anyone bold enough to step out of the shadows and be that couple for us.

Now, more than ten years after our decision to obey Him, God continues to use our story to bring hope to other struggling couples all over the world. We are cofounders of Hope & Healing Ministries, Inc., which provides resources and offers Christian peer support group for couples in adultery recovery. We have also written a book, *Unfaithful: Rebuilding Trust After Infidelity,* in which we share our story and recovery principles from a couple's point of view. Through our ministry and our book, people can see that there *is* hope for recovery from this most devastating betrayal. They too can move on to a marriage of trust and intimacy they will both cherish.

Going through the healing process was not fun. It was the hardest thing we ever did, and it cost us dearly. But it was worth it.

— Gary and Mona Shriver

∽•∾

Gary and Mona Shriver have dedicated their lives to helping broken couples find healing. You can read more of their personal journey to healing in their book, *Unfaithful: Rebuilding Trust After Infidelity.*

A few years after their own healing, Gary and Mona founded Hope & Healing Ministries, Inc., a peer ministry that provides support and healing to other survivors of marital infidelity and teaches practical strategies for working through the devastation caused by adultery. Their ministry works in partnership with a licensed Christian counselor. They also offer support groups led by couples who have themselves survived this heartbreaking experience and are dedicated to building the relationship God intended for them.

Hope & Healing Ministries, Inc.
Gary and Mona Shriver
P. O. Box 309
Denair, CA 95316
(209) 667-5012
www.hopeandhealing.us
info@hopeandhealing.us

KEN *and* NANCY

"Nancy, I'm the head of this house, and I'll decide what's best. It's not your place to question me." Ken felt his footing on this issue was biblical, supported by what he'd been taught about spiritual leadership.

A s pretty as she is, she's got to be conceited.

That's what Ken was thinking as he gazed at the seventeen-year-old, blue-eyed brunette sitting with her friends at Disneyland. Ken already knew the girl's friends, since they all frequented the same drive-in restaurant. One of them had introduced Nancy to Ken, but he kept his distance that night, figuring she was used to guys falling all over themselves for her. Still, that didn't stop him from keeping his eye on her.

About two weeks later, their plot began to unfold. The same two friends she'd been with at Disneyland drove Nancy to the drive-in restaurant. When they drove Nancy home, she ended up riding in the back seat with Ken. But this time he didn't ignore her. He glanced at her sidelong, watching her for a moment before asking, "Are you doing anything Friday night?"

Nancy was a little surprised. *So he* can *talk,* she thought. "No."

"Wanna go out?"

"Okay," she replied, smiling.

They went out that Friday night. Afterward as he drove her home, he asked her, "What are you doing tomorrow night?"

"Nothing," she said.

Encouraged, he pressed his luck. "How about Sunday?"

Again, "Nothing."

He went for the gold. "How about Monday, Tuesday, Wednesday, Thursday, Friday, Saturday, and Sunday?"

"You'll get tired of me!"

"You let me worry about that."

Ken had never felt this way about anyone. It didn't take long for him to realize she was the woman he wanted to marry. A year later, he presented her a ring in her family's living room and asked her to be his forever.

He was a nice, responsible, good-looking guy, and she was more in love than she could have imagined. She said yes. And although they both went to church, neither thought to look for "godly" traits in a spouse. They just knew they were in love.

Ken rejoiced that he would finally have a family of his own, something he had missed growing up in orphanages.

And Nancy's own happy family life made her look forward to being a wife and mother. She assumed her relationship with Ken would be much like her parents' loving relationship. Her childhood had been filled with fun family times with her parents, two sisters, and brother. There were also tons of aunts, uncles, and cousins to visit, as well as camping, sleigh riding with Dad, and a lot of love to cushion the falls that inevitably come in life. The harmony and connection that had surrounded her as a child seemed so natural that she couldn't imagine life *not* being like that. But soon her eyes were opened to a different possibility.

A BROKEN FAIRY TALE

Ever since his homeless childhood, Ken had anticipated a loving, happy family life. But nothing in his upbringing had shown him how to create one. The orphanages had been large and impersonal, the house parents impatient and intolerant. He had never known the kind of closeness Nancy took for granted.

And regretfully, the philosophy of many fundamentalist churches in those days encouraged a husband to take charge of his family—which to Ken (and multitudes of other men) meant that his family should just obey, no questions asked. So, he took charge! Nancy was expected to be the dutiful wife and wait on him hand and foot. She was also expected to clear *all* decisions through him.

Like most young girls, Nancy wanted the fairy-tale marriage. In many ways, Nancy had grown up in a "happily ever after" family and had her own idea of what the ending should look like. But now she felt like a princess locked in a lonely tower, shut away from the world and all its colors.

She began to lose touch with her beloved extended family. Ken finally had a family of his own to take care of, so he was content to stay at home, not visiting much, if at all. Her family didn't feel welcome and didn't like his dominating ways, so they rarely stopped by. It never occurred to him that his conduct was selfish and controlling. Ken sincerely threw himself into the role of the good provider, which also meant few opportunities for vacations or family outings.

Nancy says there were still some good times, but as the years passed, Ken grew more controlling. More and more he expected an unquestioning, submissive wife. They argued a lot, particularly after their first two daughters, Denise and Kristy, were born. He was very strict and a harsh disciplinarian. Although Nancy had begun developing a personal relationship with God after Denise's birth, throwing herself into Bible studies and self-help books trying to change herself to please Ken, her efforts were unsuccessful. Instead, as he became increasingly harsh and offensive, she found herself challenging him more and more as time went by.

She didn't like what she was becoming. She felt herself sinking emotionally. She figured that God was also displeased with her, but she felt a responsibility to protect her children. She became more vocal with Ken about his treatment of the girls, while becoming more demanding of *them* in an effort to avert trouble. There was no harmony, only tension.

One day, in the middle of doing laundry, Nancy heard Ken yelling at the girls again. Exasperated, she thought, *Why can't he be more like my father? He was never so harsh with us. I hate that the girls will never know what it's like to have that kind of relationship with their dad.* She set her basket down and ran down the hall to step between Ken and their youngest daughter. The tears in Kristy's eyes clinched the deal. Nancy was tired of walking on eggshells, and the girls were scared to move for fear they'd make another mistake and he would again find them unacceptable. This had to end.

Nancy turned to Ken. "I may have picked you, but the girls didn't. I guess I have to live with my choice, but they didn't have a choice, so I'm not going to let you treat them this way."

"Nancy, I'm the head of this house, and I'll decide what's best. It's not your place to question me."

Ken felt his footing on this issue was biblical, supported by what he'd been taught about spiritual leadership. And he wasn't alone. In fact, a nationally known Christian ministry based in the Midwest had asked him to join their staff. Ironically, his job would be to help strengthen families. So after thirteen years of marriage, they moved to Illinois, leaving Nancy's family and friends far behind.

They flew out two weeks before the moving van would arrive. But as soon as Ken arrived at his new job, he learned of an upcoming staff retreat. It meant he would be gone when the movers came, but he felt certain that Nancy would be supportive. That was, after all, her job.

There was a bounce in Ken's step when he walked into the kitchen after work one day. Nancy quickly wiped her eyes. It vaguely registered with him that she had been crying, but he dismissed it and launched into a spiel about his day and the upcomng retreat.

He finished, "Anyway, the retreat will be a good chance to get to know everyone and become a part of the ministry."

Nancy glared at him with red-rimmed eyes. "What am I suppose to do when the moving van gets here? You want me to stay alone for days, in the dead of winter, in a place where I don't know anyone, and then handle the move by *myself*?" She wrapped her sweater around her a little tighter in the cold kitchen.

"I have to go on this retreat. Enough said. If you don't like it, talk to my boss." Ken thought smugly of Charles, his new employer. He held a similar view of marriage. *He'll set her straight.*

"Fine. If that's what I have to do to get you to help me, I will." Nancy gave him one last frustrated look before turning to leave the kitchen.

Do You Love Her?

The next day at work Charles called Ken into his office. Charles asked Ken to skip the retreat and help Nancy with the move. Ken scarcely heard the rest of the conversation. He was too angry and mortified to listen.

He was still fuming as he walked home that day. *How can she embarrass me like this? They're going to think I can't keep my own family in line, and she's ruined my chance to be a part of this retreat. Why couldn't she just stay in her place?*

On his way home, he felt the Holy Spirit asking him a question: *Do you love her?*

No! He snapped back with such vehemence it startled him. Ken quickly rethought his answer. *I mean, of course I love her. I say it all the time.*

But the thought wouldn't leave him alone. It gnawed on him until he realized he didn't truly love Nancy. And soon he realized that he didn't even know what love was. He certainly didn't love Nancy as Christ loved her—sacrificially and unconditionally. Ken had not been putting Nancy's well-being ahead of his own. And here he was on staff with a ministry that was supposed to help marriages and families.

As he walked along, he realized that he and Nancy were in trouble. It was as if God gave him new eyes with which to look at their marriage. He saw now that he and Nancy argued constantly, and the only times she stopped looking anxious and really seemed happy were when they were around other people. He acknowledged that he would do things behind her back because she seemed to argue with whatever he did. This sure wasn't the marriage he had imagined having when he'd dreamed of life beyond the orphanage.

God, will You show me where to start?

A New Reality

At first, he kept these thoughts to himself. He was still fuming when the furniture arrived. But God continued revealing truths to Ken about his relationship. Before long, Ken had the desire to read the Bible from cover to cover for the first time ever. And as he read, he discovered messages he had never heard preached from a pulpit.

For example, he discovered that although a wife's submission to her husband is indeed listed in Scripture, true submission is actually a two-way street. He realized that to preach that women *alone* are supposed to be submissive skewed God's incredible message to the world about unselfishness—revealed within the marriage relationship. He realized that God never intended for a wife to mindlessly yield to her husband. Instead, God wants both husband and wife to clearly understand His design—to bless the husband through his wife and the wife through her husband.

God began using some humbling experiences on the job to help Ken understand his wife. His position required frequent interaction with the public. Often, these people would write him.

One day he found out he wasn't receiving any of that mail because his employer was concerned that the compliments would make him proud. He felt controlled and betrayed. When he vented his frustration to Nancy, he was taken aback by her response.

"That's exactly what you do to me."

Later, when Ken told Nancy about how he had felt devalued by some of his co-workers' actions, he was met with the same response. "That's exactly what you do to me."

It began to dawn on Ken that God was letting him go through those emotionally traumatic circumstances so he could identify with the emotions he had caused Nancy to feel. He now knew what it felt like to be controlled, betrayed, and devalued. Maybe the problem wasn't all Nancy.

Ken was changing, but Nancy wasn't yet convinced. After years of enduring Ken's negative responses and trying to remake herself for him, her heart was finally closed off. She had a hard time trusting that this new change was genuine, especially early on when he still had much to learn about how to treat her lovingly.

But Ken was determined to prove that the changes were real. Only after a year or so of steady change did she begin to really open up again. And when she finally felt safe enough to be honest with him, a barrage of anger came pouring out. Ken was totally unprepared for this. A part of him wished she would let sleeping dogs lie, but he was careful in his reaction. He didn't want to lose the rapport they had been building.

Since Ken was to be Christlike to Nancy, that meant she should be able to come to him anytime with anything and be unconditionally accepted. This wasn't limited to things that he felt were important, and it didn't mean that she could approach him only if she said things nicely. It was an invitation to total openness. If husbands were meant to mirror the love of Christ in their marriages, then he had to react to Nancy as Christ would—no matter what she said or did.

As she healed, years of bottled up emotion continued to flow out. Nothing, past or present, was left unsaid or unresolved. As her angry words were met with his loving response, the memories began to lose their power to hurt her. In listening, watching, and loving unconditionally—treating her in a Christlike fashion—Ken began to learn how to care for her and nurture her spirit.

By this time, their third daughter had been born. This was his chance to start fresh and give little Sarah the closeness he hadn't had with the other two. But he still had to work at repairing his relationship with the older girls—and there was a lot of damage in their hearts.

His chance came one day when Denise got into trouble at home. Ken and Nancy talked outside her room. He was angry, but Nancy calmly urged him to hold back. "You need to learn to care for their spirits, just as you learned to care for mine."

Ken was dumbfounded, but by now he knew to trust her judgment. "Why?"

"Because they are little women. Care for their spirits just as you do mine." Nancy laid her hand on his arm gently. "Just go in and hug her."

Ken's brows drew together, perplexed. "If I do that, she'll think I approve of what she did."

"Just hug her." Nancy smiled and gave him a little nudge.

Ken walked in to where Denise sat silently on her bed. Worry flashed across her face just before he folded her in his arms. Then she melted, responding to the love he gave freely. The healing had begun.

Later, he and Nancy sat sipping cocoa in the kitchen. "Do all women think like that?" He wondered why hugging Denise would be more constructive than concrete discipline.

Nancy grinned. "I don't know, but that's how I think."

Ken shook his head. "I guess I have a lot to learn."

He continued learning from prayer, Scripture, and his wife.

And he found that as he became more concerned about his walk with God, Nancy followed his example. They grew closer and, once again, found joy and comfort in each other's presence. The whole family became a closer, happier unit.

LAY DOWN MY *WHAT*?

Despite that, Ken went underground with his changes. In churches they had been a part of, the idea of husbands learning to "lay down their lives for their wives" was still a controversial notion — and certainly not encouraged from the pulpit. The sacrificial love that was the hallmark of Jesus' own character was too often seen as a weakness. Instead, many couples preferred to maintain the status quo, hide their hurts, and make everyone believe that life was beautiful.

Several years later, when they moved back to California, old friends saw the difference in their relationship almost immediately. This peaceful, trusting, relaxed, and happy couple bore only superficial resemblance to the Ken and Nancy they'd known before.

This couple had something those same friends wanted for themselves.

Over and over, Ken and Nancy were asked what they had done to change their relationship. Men would see the difference in Ken and ask him where the change came from. He was happy to help them, and he eventually wrote a book to walk others through the process. In seeking to love his wife, he had inadvertently found a ministry that they are still involved in twenty-five years later.

Forty-eight years into their marriage, they exude peace, love, and openness that are rare in today's world. There are still occasional problems to deal with, but nothing is swept under the rug. Nothing is too small for their attention. In fact, they believe that letting sleeping dogs lie is a recipe for failure in a marriage.

GOING PUBLIC

Ken and Nancy now have a national ministry. They have the privilege of sharing the incredible blessings derived from being obedient to God's command that a man must learn how to lay down his life for his wife. A husband should literally illustrate Christ to the person who knows him better than anyone else in the world, his wife.

Undaunted by the stir the very biblical notion of "understanding your wife" creates in some religious circles even today, Ken says, "I'd love other couples to have what we have. It is available to all couples, but not without a cost. A man must be willing to die to himself."

—*As told to Lisa Holloway*

⤳•⤶

Ken Nair is the author of the books *Discovering the Mind of a Woman* and *Discovering the Heart of a Man*. He and his wife, Nancy, are the founders of Life Partners Christian Ministries. This ministry came as a natural outgrowth of Ken's ministry to his friends, when they asked him to teach them how to apply biblical relationship principles to their own relationships.

Life Partners Discovery Seminars are offered nationwide and seek to teach men the skills they need to relate to their wives in a Christlike fashion, thus building close, happy families. Leadership training is also available, as is individual mentoring in the Mesa, Arizona area.

Life Partners Christian Ministries
10834 North 32nd Street
Phoenix, AZ 85028
(602) 485-5115
www.lifepartners.org
ken@lifepartners.org
nancy@lifepartners.org

Ramiro was stuck in a line of slow-moving traffic. His anxiety grew as he moved closer to the accident that caused the delay. Finally, as his van pushed forward to the scene of the accident — his fears were confirmed.

Six years into their marriage, the stresses of life were piling up for Lupe and Ramiro. They already had three children — seven-year-old Miro, five-year-old Julian, and four-year-old Gabbie — and their limited income relegated them to a crowded apartment in a high-crime area. The kids couldn't play outside without strict supervision.

So when the opportunity arose to move into a brand-new four-bedroom house on a forested acre adjacent to the White Mountain Apache reservation, where Lupe spent her childhood, Lupe jumped at the chance. The house would be provided by Lupe's tribe, so they could easily afford the move. She knew their children would benefit from the clean mountain air, the space to run, and the close proximity to her extended family on the reservation. She hoped Ramiro would be able to find a job — there was a furniture business in the area, and furniture delivery was his specialty.

Ramiro went out to apply at the furniture store and was immediately hired. Less than a month after being approved for a house in the Apache Dawn subdivision in Hon Dah, Arizona, the Canaleses moved into their new home.

It seemed like a good move for the family. Three weeks after being hired by the local furniture store, Ramiro was promoted to a position in management. They spent that year's Thanksgiving holiday in the joyful presence of Lupe's extended family. Life in the mountains was idyllic, almost dreamlike. Finally, the Canales family had the home for which little Miro and Julian had prayed, one in which the kids could run free around their house. Everyone was healthy and happy. It was a new beginning for the Canales family.

A Storm Approaches

The first weekend of December marked the start of the Christmas season. The family prepared for the coming holiday by decorating their new home, shopping for Christmas lights, and driving around to look at neighbors' Christmas displays. They strung lights on the house, set up their Christmas tree in front of the picture window in their new living room, and trimmed the tree with ornaments.

Ramiro bought and chopped firewood while Lupe and the kids stacked it high. Soon snow began to fall, and the family delighted in watching the fragile white flakes descend on their cozy new home. That Saturday night, all five family members — Mom, Dad, Miro, Julian, and Gabbie — slept cuddled together on the floor of their living room in front of a crackling fire.

It was the last weekend the couple spent with little Miro and Julian.

On Monday, December 8, 2003, a snowstorm hit Hon Dah. Since the Canaleses shared one car, Lupe drove Ramiro to work that morning and got home before the snow hit hard. Around noon, Ramiro thought about calling Lupe to ask if she'd bring their car to him at work. He planned to use his lunch hour to drive her home so she wouldn't have to worry about picking him up later on. The guys at work had warned him about the dangers of driving in mountain snow.

Ramiro lifted up the phone, poised to dial home. Then he remembered that Lupe had to do laundry that day, and since she didn't have her own washer and dryer yet, she would be at the laundromat. He put the phone down, ate his lunch, and went back to work.

Later that evening, as the snow fell harder, Lupe cooked dinner for the family. She set the table; bundled the kids in their pajamas, slippers, and winter coats; and piled everyone in the car to go pick up Ramiro from work. Little Miro wanted to sit on the front passenger side, as he always did when his dad wasn't in the car. Julian sat behind Miro, and Gabbie sat behind Lupe. After Lupe had everyone strapped in, she checked her rearview mirror. The kids were excited about driving through the snow.

The furniture store was thirteen miles from their home. Lupe drove slowly and cautiously through the dense snow. Soon the snow was so heavy that she could no longer see the lines on the road. A procession of cars inched along slowly, but Lupe's car picked up speed as they drove down an icy hill.

That's the last thing Lupe remembers about that night.

Ramiro checked the time. It was six o'clock. Lupe usually arrived ten minutes early to pick up her husband from work. Ramiro shivered as he stood in front of the building, wondering where his wife was. He saw an ambulance screech by. Then another. Then yet another. He prayed that those emergency vehicles had nothing to do with his wife being late. "Lord, I hope they're okay."

Ramiro's boss offered to let him to borrow the company van to get home. "If your wife doesn't come by, just bring the van back in the morning," he said. Anxiously, Ramiro got in the van and drove down the main strip toward his home. Soon Ramiro was stuck in a line of slow-moving traffic. His anxiety grew as he moved closer to the accident that caused the delay. Finally, as his van pushed forward to the scene of the accident, his fears were confirmed.

There, just ahead, was his car — crushed and lit eerily by the flashing lights of police cars and fire trucks. Ramiro jumped out of the van, slipping on the snow and ice. He collapsed onto the pavement and screamed, "This isn't happening!"

A police officer at the scene told Ramiro that his wife and children had already been transported to area hospitals. The officer took him to the hospital.

A hospital official approached Ramiro when he arrived. "I need to talk to you privately."

She told him Miro and Julian had been killed in the accident.

Ramiro was in a state of shock. But he had no time to grapple with his emotions. He had to immediately board a helicopter to transport his severely injured daughter to a hospital in Phoenix. Lupe would be flown out fifteen minutes later.

During the week following the accident, Lupe drifted in and out of consciousness, often asking for her children. The hospital staff told her that her sons had been killed in the accident. But because she'd had a traumatic brain injury and had experienced short-term memory loss, the news didn't register. Each time they told her, she experienced the agonizing blow all over again. It was just the beginning of a long and difficult journey that lay before the bereaved mother.

Ramiro learned later that Lupe's car slipped on "black ice"—transparent, partially melted ice on blacktop. Driving down a hill, Lupe's car hit a patch of the unusually slick ice, spun around three times, and slid into oncoming traffic, where it collided full force with another car.

Their daughter, Gabbie, was briefly hospitalized for injuries to the right side of her head. Four days after the accident, and with Lupe still hospitalized, little Gabbie accompanied a devastated Ramiro to bury his only sons, Miro and Julian, on the reservation.

Ramiro resigned from his job at the furniture company. Their new house sat untouched.

RECOVERING

Lupe was released from the hospital on December 24, 2003, six-teen days after the accident. But she had a long road of intense physical, occupational, and speech therapy ahead. After spending Christmas in California with extended family, she and Ramiro moved in with Ramiro's brother, Joe, and his family in Phoenix. They stayed in Joe's garage. Financially, it seemed their only option. They needed a cheap place to stay. Ramiro couldn't work because he had to be around to care for his wife and daughter.

As for their new house in Hon Dah, they returned four months later and moved everything out, giving away most of their belong-ings. They sold the house and returned to Phoenix to live with Joe and his family.

As happens with many couples who suffer the loss of a child, the Canaleses began to blame themselves — and one another — for the loss of their sons.

Ramiro blamed Lupe for letting her desire to be closer to family and for a house push them to move to the reservation. If they hadn't moved, maybe their boys would still be with them. Maybe if Lupe had been more careful while driving, the accident wouldn't have happened. Lupe blamed Ramiro. If only he had called her and taken the car from her during his lunch break, the boys wouldn't have died.

Living in cramped quarters didn't help. Although Lupe and Ramiro were grateful for the hospitality of Joe and his family, stay-ing in their garage room caused them to squabble over the lack of space and the stifling lack of privacy. Lupe wanted to move right away so she could be alone with what was left of her family and recover in the privacy of her own home.

But Ramiro hoped to take things slowly and was happy to live in his brother's garage for as long as possible. With Ramiro not working, they had no choice but to stay put.

After a while, Lupe couldn't handle their restricted life in the garage any longer. On several occasions Lupe threw up her arms in frustration and moved into her mom's place for weeks at a time. For Lupe, divorce seemed like a normal, even comfortable, means of escape. Her mother and father had divorced when she was a kid, and she was raised by a single mother. She knew she could handle the life of a single mom.

Conflict between Lupe and Ramiro was nothing new. It had taken root early in their marriage. Ramiro's Latino upbringing emphasized male dominance, macho-man virility, and moral authority as the head of the household. His expectation was that he and his wife's roles would be defined according to traditional Latino culture. Lupe, conversely, had been brought up in a single-mother Native American household that emphasized a strong matriarchy as an efficient family structure. Their conflicting views of male and female roles caused the couple to butt heads frequently.

Early in their marriage, when her conflicts with Ramiro had intensified, Lupe had sought refuge in the arms of another man.

And yet, each time Lupe and Ramiro had separated, they had always ended up reuniting. Ramiro wished to salvage his marriage, and he always wanted to talk things through with his wife. Although Lupe would refuse to speak with Ramiro for a while, every time they separated, both before and after their sons died, Ramiro would ask Lupe to come back, and she'd return.

It was during one of their separations, in October of 2004, almost a year after the accident, that Ramiro and Lupe signed up for a conference held by the National Association of Marriage Enhancement (NAME) in a final effort to save their marriage. Ramiro had heard about NAME, a faith-based marriage ministry, through an announcement at their church. If their marriage had any chance of survival, Ramiro told Lupe, she needed to go to the conference with him. Lupe agreed to go.

THE TURNING POINT

Several things helped the Canaleses reconcile during and after the NAME conference. One thing that affected them was when another couple at the conference shared a startling statistic: close to 90 percent of couples who have lost a child end up divorcing. When Lupe and Ramiro heard this statistic, they looked at each other in astonishment. "We lost *two*," Lupe said to Ramiro. "Can you imagine the statistics on us?" Rather than discouraging them, though, hearing this statistic made them all the more determined — they wanted to beat the odds, not only for their living daughter but also for their deceased sons. They wanted them to have not died in vain.

Another thing that impacted them during the conference was an exercise in which leaders asked participants to look in each other's eyes and forgive one another. As Lupe and Ramiro gazed at each other and said the words, "I forgive you," healing tears began to flow.

At the conference the couple learned that praying together is a powerful way to strengthen a marriage. So from that point forward, Lupe and Ramiro began saying a small prayer together every night. This, they say, is the glue that has held them together over the last few years.

The Canaleses also learned at the NAME conference that if they were serious about staying together, divorce could no longer be an option for them. At the conference, NAME founder Pastor Leo Godzich addressed the participants: "I want you couples to stand up, and as you look at each other, I want you to say 'I will never talk about divorce again.'" This small piece of advice helped

Lupe and Ramiro's resolve to stay together. Although they had frequently discussed divorce in the past, from then on they stopped talking about it completely.

At the conference Lupe and Ramiro learned the importance of fellowship. While they lived with Joe's family, they tried to stay out of the way as much as possible, to keep to themselves. But NAME encouraged them to meet other couples, to get to know other members of their community. Doing so helped them learn that other couples had overcome heartbreaking situations and had maintained loving, lasting relationships. "If God can help those couples," Lupe and Ramiro said to themselves, "He can do the same for us."

The conference empowered them to make positive changes in their relationship and in their lives. So they made a promise to each other and to God that they wouldn't separate again. By the conference's end that Sunday in October of 2004, Lupe and Ramiro had a new resolve to stay together, to work through their problems, and to help others do the same. They've been together ever since.

A major reason that couples who suffer the loss of a child divorce is because of guilt and blame. Parents blame themselves, and then they shift the blame to their partners. Lupe and Ramiro were no different. But it wasn't until they took the advice of Pastor Tommy Barnett, of Phoenix First Assembly, that they decided to stop blaming one another for their sons' death. "When it's a person's time to go, that's it," the pastor counseled them. "There's nothing anyone can do to change it. When it's your time, you'll go. It's not anyone's fault."

At that moment Ramiro and Lupe realized that December 8, 2003, was Miro and Julian's time to go. They could finally let go of the guilt and the blame and make peace with their boys' death—and with one another.

Now, Lupe and Ramiro are deeply involved with the NAME ministry. They serve as a care couple, counseling other struggling married couples. Because of the tragedy and recovery in their marriage, they are often called upon to counsel families who have lost a child.

MOVING FORWARD

Today, people all over the world have heard the Canaleses' story. "We're living proof," they tell people, "that God is real and that He is able to restore and to love."

Holidays and birthdays remain challenging for them as they continue to grieve the death of their boys. But since that October in 2004, the Canales family has had much to celebrate. After living with Joe's family for several months, they were finally able to move into their own apartment near their beloved church, Phoenix First Assembly.

Now, Lupe and Ramiro both have good jobs. Ramiro drives a delivery truck, and Lupe works with Native American students in a literacy lab. The couple and their daughter, Gabbie, finally moved into their first house since Miro and Julian went "home." Ramiro and Lupe find a great deal of encouragement in their daily life — encouragement from their daughter, Gabbie, wise beyond her years, from their friends at church, from the knowledge that their boys are safe in God's arms, and from the love they share with one another now that they have recommitted to their relationship.

Just three months before 7-year-old Miro died, his parents overheard him praying. They heard him ask God for a home of his own, and for Daddy to love Mommy. Soon after, God provided his family with a beautiful home in the mountains. The two short months he spent there with his family were the happiest of his life. But now, through his death, his prayers have truly been answered.

He and his brother are living with Jesus in their eternal home, and Daddy loves Mommy more than ever.

—As told to Heather Zydek

☙ • ❧

Lupe and Ramiro Canales attended a NAME conference soon after losing their two sons in a tragic accident. This conference helped keep their marriage intact.

NAME founders Dr. Leo and Molly Godzich travel nationwide offering conferences, seminars, resource materials, and training for congregations that want to start a NAME counseling center. Because NAME counseling is given by couples to couples, it offers a safe haven for healing and a new beginning.

NAME centers have been established all over the country. NAME also has a "marriage-mobile" that travels to under-served communities where social stresses are destroying family life. NAME offers free premarital workshops, as well as crisis counseling, communication skills training, anger and money management programs, and more.

NAME (National Association of Marriage Enhancement)
Dr. Leo and Molly Godzich
P. O. Box 30777
Phoenix, AZ 85046
(888) 262-NAME
www.nameonline.net
info@nameonline.net

JONATHAN *and* ELAINE

*Secrets, I discovered, are deadly. The longer I indulged my
secret sexual addiction, the nearer I drew to death's door. The
shame was unbearable, but the only way I knew to numb the
pain was to medicate it sexually.*

I clearly remember the moment I met her. It was a hot August
day in 1994. I was a junior in college and she was a freshman.
I had decided to go to a campus ministries progressive dinner to
"check out" the incoming students for that semester. I had no idea
what I was in for that night.

I filled my plate and then turned to find a seat. The room was
packed with college students gearing up for the coming months
of study and mayhem. I walked toward a table and stopped short
when I saw her. She was smiling, laughing at something someone
at the table had just said. Her captivating brown eyes caught me
off guard. They danced as she laughed. I quickly grabbed a seat
across from her and her friend, introduced myself, and began the
rest of my life.

Shortly after our potluck introduction we began dating. Elaine
was full of life and depth, and she had a gentle warmth about her
that drew people in like a magnet. I was rapidly falling in love with
her and she with me. There was only one problem. I had a secret—a
big one. But I chose not to reveal it because I was certain it would
crush our budding love. That was a risk I wasn't willing to take.

I had carried my secret from the time I was twelve years old. At that time I was introduced to pornography by a friend while play-ing in the woods behind his house. While exploring, my friend led me to an open field with an old, hollowed-out tree stump in the middle of it. In that tree stump was a *Playboy* magazine. After only a few minutes of gazing at those pictures, pornography had sunk its hooks deep into my soul.

All throughout junior high and high school I privately fed my hunger for porn and the rush it would supply. My life soon became that of a divided man, outwardly appearing to be a duti-ful Christian, yet inwardly decaying through my repeated failures against the beast of lust. I was filled with shame but unable to muster the courage to expose my secret to anyone, especially not to a girl I was falling so desperately for.

After only a few months of dating I was convinced Elaine was "the one." While visiting her in San Antonio during the Christmas holiday break, I told her of my love for her. I won't lie—I was ner-vous. But I was certain of my feelings for her. So when we were alone one evening, I told Elaine I loved her. She, however, did not echo the sentiment. I was a bit stunned when my sincere "I love you" was not met with one in return. She explained that she had never told a guy she loved him because she was reserving that statement for the one man she would choose to marry. She wasn't certain I was that man, but she said I didn't have any marks against me so far.

Eventually, Elaine did tell me she loved me. I had already chosen her, but now she was choosing me. I knew how much her "I love you" meant. Before long, we were making wedding plans.

But I still had this secret. The guilt of carrying it was weighing heavily on our relationship. I felt that if I didn't share something with Elaine about my secret that I would be engaging in a kind of marriage fraud. My future wife deserved to know. So I finally confessed to her that I wasn't a virgin, which was part, but not all, of the ugly truth.

That conversation began a very painful period in our dating. My confession didn't match up with the dreams Elaine had of her knight in shining armor coming to sweep her off her feet. But through her disappointment, she couldn't deny her love for me, and the wedding plans continued.

The wedding was exhilarating, and it seemed to provide a fresh start, especially for me. I naïvely believed that Elaine was the cure to my sexual addiction. I thought she would remove my lustfulness by being there for me sexually and emotionally. I didn't realize at the time that my problem had nothing to do with Elaine. She wasn't the cause of it, and she couldn't possibly be the solution to it. But I chose to believe the fantasy anyway.

As happens with all fantasy, reality eventually bursts the bubble. Several months into our marriage, after the honeymoon faded, I found myself drawn back into my private, divided self. The secret called out to me and I answered. At first, it was seemingly innocent behaviors like masturbating in the shower or allowing sexual fantasies to play out in my mind. But I rapidly grew bored with those outlets. I craved more.

One day Elaine came home from work to discover me playing with my newest toy: a computer. Her expression was a mixture of shock and confusion, like she had missed out on something that should have been a joint venture. You see, I hadn't talked with her about it. I'd just decided I wanted it, so I had bought it with a credit card. Three thousand dollars got me a spiffy new computer and a less-than-thrilled wife.

Soon after I bought the computer I was connected to the Internet and conducting secret pornographic searches, all the while ensuring that Elaine knew nothing about my online habits. I would erase page histories to make everything appear to be "above board." Even though Elaine didn't know exactly what I was doing online, she did know that I was spending a *lot* of time on the computer—so much time, in fact, that she nicknamed the computer "Jezebel." She would later learn how appropriate that name really was.

The deeper I dove into my secret, the more frustrated, divided, and ashamed I became. But my frustrations were aimed in the wrong direction. Rather than harboring animosity or hatred for the behaviors I was engaging in, I directed my anger at Elaine. I convinced myself that the marriage itself was to blame for my discomfort.

After only eighteen months of marriage, I left. Bolted, really. I didn't tell Elaine why I was leaving or where I was going. I just packed up my tiny Ford Escort and drove. Eventually, I landed at a friend's house in Nashville. I was a confused, empty, angry, and terrified wreck. I felt like I was losing my mind, but I didn't know what to do about it.

I was gone for nearly three weeks, trying to convince myself that getting out was the best thing for me. I told myself I would blaze my own trail, drop the dead weight, and live life on my own terms. But my gut ached like some living thing was gnawing at me from the inside trying to escape. Unable to cope, I dragged my broken self back to Texas, back to Elaine, truly wanting a fresh start. Remarkably, Elaine warmly welcomed me home, and we agreed to fight for the marriage.

We went to a few counseling sessions soon after my return, but they didn't help. It was like trying to dam Niagara Falls by tossing a twig in the water. Within just six months I was back on the computer hunting porn. Except this time I discovered a new wrinkle: online chat.

Up to this point in our marriage, all of my addictive behaviors had been self-directed, meaning I would simply look at porn and masturbate or fantasize. There hadn't been any involvement with another person. But chat changed all that. It allowed me to engage in sexual fantasies with a real person on the other end. This heightened the rush for me because it increased the risk. I reached a new plateau of sexual addiction, one that would soon prove to be my undoing.

For the first few years of our marriage Elaine was frustrated and confused by me. All my behaviors were secretive. *All* of them. She didn't know the details of what I was doing online or elsewhere. Even when I fled to Nashville she didn't fully know my reasons. I kept all my thoughts and emotions bottled up inside. Her frustration grew as I became more distant and detached. She craved attention from me, some sign that I still loved her and wanted her — that I still thought she was beautiful. To her, our marriage seemed like a puzzle. But the puzzle lacked a few pieces. Her heart grew cold and fragile as I pushed her further and further away.

Secrets, I discovered, are deadly. The longer I indulged my secret sexual addiction, the nearer I drew to death's door. The shame was unbearable, but the only way I knew to numb the pain was to medicate it sexually. Therefore, as my turmoil increased, so did my destructive behaviors, and I became more irrational and dangerous. I eventually met one of the chat room women in person for unprotected sex. That first encounter, as thrilling and terrifying as it was, opened up a world of sexual sin that later forced me to my knees.

After the chat room affair, I felt any semblance of hope disappear; unbearable emptiness was all that remained. But I still wasn't ready to surrender to God. Over the next six months I engaged in multiple sexual affairs with anonymous individuals I met online. Each encounter was an attempt to medicate the growing numbness of my emotional and spiritual self. With each affair I felt myself crawling closer and closer to death, as if I could hear the nails being pounded into my coffin with each act of infidelity.

The bottom fell out in the summer of 1999. My secret was

finally exposed. Elaine had grown increasingly suspicious of my behaviors, especially since I was spending less time at home in the evenings due to my sexual escapades. As her suspicions grew, I couldn't make up enough excuses or cover all the lies. And, honestly, I was tired of carrying the secret. The weight of it bent me to the floor. Under this weight, I decided to approach Elaine and tell what I had been hiding.

So one evening, I blindsided Elaine and told her everything. Needless to say, that was a long, excruciating night. The tension was immense. Like a machine, I rattled off all my infidelities, all the lies, all the secrets. I grew numb in the telling. I wasn't even concerned that Elaine was crumbling to the floor in front of me as her dream world of a marriage built on honesty and integrity collided with the reality that her husband was a sex addict.

I wish I could say the sky parted, the sun shone down on us, and everything was perfect from that point on. Hardly. Within a week of my confession I was in bed with another woman. The confession alone hadn't set me free. When I came home from that sexual encounter Elaine met me at the door with her bags packed. She knew where I had been and what I had done. It was over. She said she was leaving and didn't want to see me again. The door closed. The silence was deafening as I sat alone on the couch in our now very empty house.

Back From the Dead

Little did Elaine know that her leaving me would be the catalyst for change I needed in my life. It looked like my marriage was dead. And that was the picture of death I needed to realize the magnitude of my sin. I had finally reached rock-bottom. I was broken — *truly* broken. I wondered if God could still love me, if He even wanted to heal me and lead me to true freedom. Shame consumed me and kept my face to the floor.

But in the still silence of that day God met me. He met me on the floor, though I was covered in the filth of years of shame and sin. I distinctly remember two words that kept coming to mind over and over as I cried: *grace* and *hope*.

I had never felt such tenderness and grace in all my life as I did on that day. I poured out my heart to God. I confessed my sin. As I confessed, I fully expected to receive wrath and judgment from God. But instead I felt a shower — no, a downpour — of grace wash over me. It was as if God breathed a sigh of relief on my behalf and whispered, "Jonathan, I have waited so long for this day. I accept your humility and brokenness. I will heal you if you'll let Me."

God filled my spirit with a freshness, a glimmer of light at the end of a very long tunnel. While I was still far from that light, I knew God was offering me a new future, a new life. I smiled, face-down in a puddle of my own tears, amazed that God would give such a wonderful gift to someone so unworthy.

I prayed passionately for Elaine that day, that her heart was not beyond repair and that she could know God's love and comfort. I didn't know what the future held for our marriage; I knew only that I wanted God to touch Elaine as He had touched me. I wasn't even concentrating on the restoration of our marriage in that moment. My heart truly broke for Elaine and the pain she had endured because of me. That day began a nine-month separation during which the shattered pieces of our broken marriage were sifted through and the seeds of new life were planted.

God began doing amazing things in my life. I connected with a good counselor and began peeling back the layers covering my years of secrecy and habitual lying. I began to embrace the unconditional, unending love and grace of God. I began to set safe boundaries in my life. I gave up TV, and for over two years I gave up the Internet at home. I made myself vulnerable to people in the church and to a weekly accountability group—a group I still meet with to this day. In those difficult months of separation, I finally began to understand what it means to live a life of purity.

Every day while we were separated, I sent a letter to Elaine, sharing with her the changes God was making in my life. Elaine never responded to those letters, but that was fine by me. I just wanted her to see into my heart, to see the work going on inside. I was becoming a totally different person. My heart was softening. I was no longer afraid to be known, dirty secrets and all. In this transformation, I began to learn how to really love Elaine. This frightened me, because I had no idea if there was hope for our broken marriage. I knew God was capable of saving our marriage; I just didn't know if Elaine would be willing to give me another chance.

But God was working on Elaine during our separation as well. He created a new compassion in her heart for me and others ensnared in sexually addictive patterns. He showed her some of her own faults and unfaithfulness to Him. He helped her discover anew His forgiveness for her—and He created a desire in her heart to forgive me. It was God who produced a miracle and saved our shattered marriage.

On April 8, 2000, Elaine and I went back to that big white church where we'd been married. We walked back down the aisle and renewed our vows. Then I moved back into the house, and we began our journey toward true intimacy and a union based on hope, honesty, love, and faith.

God has heaped blessings on us, confirming His goodness in our lives. He has given us three precious children, who are continual reminders of His grace. He has also given us the great gift of sharing the promise of purity and freedom to thousands struggling with sexual addiction around the world through Be Broken Ministries. This privilege brings unspeakable joy to our lives as we continually see God do for others what He did for us.

By the way, Elaine saved all the letters.

—Jonathan Daugherty

⚬●⚬

Jonathan Daugherty is the founder and director of Be Broken Ministries. Be Broken exists to offer hope and healing to sexually broken individuals. They offer books, workbooks, newsletters, articles, support groups, and counselor referrals.

Jonathan is also a host of *Pure Sex Radio*, a weekly radio program that tackles the tough issues of porn, lust, and sexual addiction and gives practical principles for living every day in sexual purity.

Be Broken Ministries, Inc.
1800 NE Loop 410, Suite 415
San Antonio, TX 78217
(800) 49-PURITY
www.bebroken.com
www.puresexradio.com
jonathan@bebroken.com

*Tim broke and Rebecca attempted to fix. Rebecca harped and
Tim hid. And so the cycle went, for two decades and through
the births of three sons.*

"Get a divorce."

That was the advice of one pastor Tim and Rebecca
Hart consulted. Another suggested they needed professional help
at the least.

Rebecca and Tim's rocky relationship was stuck in a passive-
aggressive cycle of miscommunication. Over the years they would
fight, cut, and attack each other. But when neither one could
change the other, they would back down, bury their resentments,
and go back to coexisting—never resolving their issues.

Not even a serious car accident was enough to jolt life into
their dying marriage.

After seventeen years of marriage, the Harts hit a particularly
low point and separated. A few days into the separation, Rebecca
was driving through a rainstorm when her car hydroplaned and
collided head-on with another vehicle. When she regained consciousness, all Rebecca could think about was finding her husband
to tell him she was sorry and that she loved him.

It took that kind of awakening to make her want to reconcile with him. Heartfelt communication was difficult for Rebecca.
She tended to bury her emotions underneath layers of distrust and
anger directed at her husband. But in her desperate state she found

herself wanting to reach out again to Tim.

The accident's impact was severe. Rebecca suffered a punctured lung and broken ribs. Every bone in her face was broken, so the doctors performed immediate facial and eye surgery. While recovering, she had to breathe through a tracheal tube, and her jaw was wired shut. Her eyes were still recovering too, so she couldn't see. The nine days Rebecca spent incapacitated in a hospital bed seemed like an eternity.

Tim, who in the past had often proved unreliable, this time rose to the occasion. He rushed to his wife's side and tended to her needs. He acted as her eyes and ears while she was in the hospital, and then for several weeks at home.

For a time it seemed that this accident had given Tim and Rebecca the wake-up call their marriage had needed. They came to see how precious and fleeting life is, and they clung to one another. For the three months following the accident, the couple spent a lot of quality time together. They even *talked*, something they hadn't really done in years.

But little by little, as Rebecca recovered, their rekindled love and reliance on one another faded, and she and Tim returned to a sense of normalcy. They reverted to their old ways of taking one another for granted, miscommunicating, and allowing resentment to fester unchecked.

A LOOK BACK

Tim had first noticed Rebecca when they were in middle school together. Back then, Tim was scruffy-headed and shy. He admired Rebecca from a distance until high school, when he finally worked up the nerve to approach her at a party and ask for her phone number.

The next day, rather than calling her, he and some friends drove to Rebecca's suburban neighborhood in Tim's dilapidated car. Rebecca wasn't home, but her father was working in the yard when Tim and his friends pulled up. Rebecca's father was alarmed at the sight of this car filled with rough-looking, longhaired boys and their girlfriends. When Tim approached Rebecca's father to ask if his daughter was home, her father bluntly forbade Tim from ever trying to see Rebecca again.

But Rebecca was drawn to Tim. He had a kind heart, and she liked the way he talked about his feelings. She even liked his flaws. Rebecca was a fixer, and Tim seemed like a worthy project.

Soon the pair began dating, despite Rebecca's parents' objection to their relationship. They began sneaking around. To keep Rebecca's parents from catching on, Tim had one of his clean-cut friends arrive at the house to pick Rebecca up for dates. Then this friend would hand her off to Tim, and she and Tim would spend the evening together. This continued all through high school.

Though the two were drawn to one another, their relationship quickly grew tumultuous. Between parties and good times they would often fight, break up, reconcile, and break up again.

One recurring theme in their conflict involved Tim's jealousy of Rebecca's active social life. Tim was a warm-hearted loner from a broken home. Rebecca had loads of friends and a secure home life. Tim wanted to talk about his feelings, but Rebecca would close up when it came to sharing hers. She was drawn to Tim's ability to connect on this level, but she never found the ability to open up, which made real communication increasingly difficult in the years to come.

Their breakups were usually very brief, sometimes as short as a few hours. But right after high school they broke up and stayed apart for nearly a year. Tim wanted to marry Rebecca, but she feared her parents wouldn't approve of her decision to spend her life with a boy from the wrong side of town. So she turned him down.

But almost a year later, Rebecca and Tim decided to give it

another go. Tim asked Rebecca's father for permission to marry his daughter. This time he consented. Finally, with the blessing of Rebecca's once-skeptical father, Tim and Rebecca married.

The honeymoon didn't last long, however. Just one year into their marriage Rebecca was already contemplating divorce. Tim had grown up in an unstable, alcoholic home with few expectations or boundaries. He was used to coming and going as he pleased. So he thought nothing of leaving for a hunting trip one Friday without bothering to tell his young wife. Nor did he think it necessary to call her during the five days he was gone. Rebecca was worried sick. She had no idea where he was.

When Tim walked in the door almost a week later, he expected Rebecca to be happy to see him. Instead, she was livid. Tim was irritated with Rebecca for demanding to know where he had been and why he hadn't called. Rebecca was devastated by Tim's lack of consideration and his apparent lack of common sense.

The hunting trip gone awry was just the tip of the iceberg for the newlyweds. They found themselves constantly at odds. Tim worked too many hours, or so Rebecca thought. Rebecca's social life was too active, or so Tim thought. Tim was too loose with the money he earned. Rebecca was too thrifty and worried too much over what she considered unwise expenditures.

Then, when Rebecca started having children, she stopped partying. Now Tim felt betrayed by Rebecca's new resolve not to party alongside him. Rebecca was too strict with the kids. Tim wasn't strict enough. Rebecca martyred herself. Tim buried himself in alcohol and excuses. Tim broke and Rebecca attempted to fix. Rebecca harped and Tim hid. And so the cycle went, for two decades and through the births of three sons.

After many years as foreman at a manufacturing company, Tim resigned from his position to start his own business with friends. Rebecca warned Tim not to leave his job or get involved with this

venture. She didn't believe he had done adequate research to prepare for such an endeavor, and she didn't trust his business partners. Tim ignored Rebecca's pleas. He relied on his own impulses
and hoped to prove her wrong.

Months later, the business failed, and Tim found himself dig-
ging his way out of corporate bankruptcy. Tim and his partners
closed the company and gave all of their assets to the IRS. With
two small children and another on the way, Rebecca and Tim
both had to take any kind of work they could find to keep their
family financially afloat. This kind of financial hardship is a strain
on the strongest of marriages. It was a deep wound to the Harts'
relationship. And it didn't help that Rebecca had told him not to
do it.

Eventually Tim was contacted by his previous employer,
who asked him to return to the company. Finally, with the worst
financial hardship behind them, the Harts' conflicts over the
failed business fizzled and they returned to their usual mode of
resentful tolerance. Tim and Rebecca more or less coexisted, each
going his or her own way. The model worked well enough to keep
them complacent about their marriage for several years while the
kids grew.

But once their two oldest sons left home as young adults,
something happened that caused years of buried anger to begin
to surface. The Harts' youngest son, then in high school, got into
some trouble, which triggered the couple to seek help from a pastor
at their church.

In one session their pastoral counselor shook her head. "It
doesn't make sense that your son would do this," she told them.
"There has to be more to this story. How are things at home?"

Her question opened a door that had been nailed shut for
years. And the further that door was opened, the more Rebecca
and Tim didn't like what they saw. Still, when it came to making

changes, they were both stuck in their ways, unsure of how to improve their relationship.

"GET A DIVORCE"

The pastor asked Rebecca and Tim to fill out a compatibility questionnaire, the kind of document engaged couples typically complete as part of their premarital counseling.

Rebecca filled out her questionnaire the moment she got home that night. But on the drive home, Tim threw his in the backseat, where it remained untouched.

At the next session, Rebecca walked in with her completed questionnaire. Tim came in empty-handed. "I was busy at work and didn't have time," he said. "I'll get around to it."

But at the next session, and the next, it still wasn't done. Finally Rebecca tore her questionnaire to pieces, furious at Tim's indifference. Tim fought back, saying that Rebecca was out to sabotage his efforts by refusing to allow him enough time to do his part.

When their counselor learned what had happened, she threw up her hands. "You guys are way too far gone for me. Unless you have about twenty years to wait for Tim to change, you need to get a divorce."

Rebecca was devastated. She began throwing around the D-word, hoping her ultimatums would shock Tim into making a permanent change for the better. But rather than improving, things continued to unravel.

At this point, Tim began to panic. He started attending church apart from his family, going to two or three services on a Sunday. He went from church to church, seeking counsel from pastor after pastor, desperate for someone to fix him and the situation, but not willing put in the hard work of changing himself from the inside out. Externally, he tried to fix things at home by doing extra housework and chores. But internally, he didn't know where to start. His efforts were sincere but misguided. And Rebecca wasn't impressed.

About a year into their search for help, Tim and Rebecca went to yet another pastor for advice.

He too was stumped. "Oh, man," he said. "I've never seen anybody like you two. You need *professional* help."

The Harts continued to see counselors for a year and a half before one Christian counselor recommended that they try an innovative new program called "The Third Option." The program involves free, ongoing group sessions for struggling married couples who often see only two options to marital unhappiness: endurance or divorce. The "third option" is restoration.

The program combines three components: a support group, a time of sharing by mentor couples whose once-rocky marriages have been healed, and workshops that teach relationship skills. The Harts, in need of serious reconciliation after decades of conflict, enrolled in the very first Third Option class offered in their town, hoping for the best. Rebecca was hoping for a miracle.

In the first Third Option workshop, each spouse was handed three note cards. They were to use one note card to answer each of the following questions: "What do you like about your spouse?" "What things do you want to change about your spouse?" "What can you do to change yourself and your contribution to the relationship to make it better?"

Rebecca filled up a whole note card with things she didn't like about Tim. So when the Third Option leaders asked the participants to tear up that particular note card and throw it away, Rebecca was furious.

That first class and the following meetings continue to awaken volatile feelings in Rebecca. She would often cry and scream during the fifteen-minute drive home from the sessions, feeling cheated after realizing how awful her married life truly was and how much she had lost after years of living unhappily married to Tim. Ready to give up, she gave Tim one final ultimatum: "If I don't see a change in you by June, I am filing for divorce."

Tim still wanted to resuscitate their marriage, but his actions didn't show it. He continued to make unrealistic promises, saying what he thought Rebecca wanted to hear—but he never seemed to follow through. He didn't know how to make the kind of changes that would truly mend their relationship.

As the Third Option workshops drew to a close, Rebecca's June divorce deadline was fast approaching. The Harts spent long nights loudly hashing out the dirty details of their miserable marriage. While attending Third Option, they continued to see a professional Christian counselor. One night, as they were about to leave for a counseling session, Rebecca suddenly announced she wasn't going. She said she didn't see the point anymore. So Tim went by himself.

As Tim began to talk with the counselor, suddenly Rebecca showed up and asked to talk to the counselor alone. It was then that the miracle Rebecca had been hoping for occurred—just not quite in the way she expected.

During that session she finally realized that Tim was not the source of all their problems. She realized that she had contributed to the destruction of their marriage by making it her responsibility to "fix" Tim. At that session, she let it all flow out, like water over a dam. She released years of anger, doubt, frustration, and disappointment, finally understanding that the only person she could change was herself.

In letting go of the role of "fixer," Rebecca was finally able to forgive, to move on, and to accept Tim as he was.

While Rebecca's change came in the form of an *aha!* moment, Tim's change was more gradual. In Third Option, Tim had been moved and challenged by the personal stories of the mentor couples. He also continued going to the Christian counselor, who encouraged him to be a man of character and to keep his word. In an effort to be accountable for his words and actions, Tim began taking notes during conversations with Rebecca so he would remember what he had said and promises he had made. Over time, he began to understand the importance of integrity, consistency, and responsibility.

REBUILDING

Though Tim and Rebecca were doing much better, they knew their own history. In an effort not to fall back into their old habits, the couple decided to go through the Third Option program a second time. And whenever they noticed themselves moving back into their dysfunctional cycle of codependency, they would stop and pray for God to help them get back on track. They were accustomed to fighting, so they had to learn new ways of communicating. *Not fighting* felt strange, but eventually they learned to attack the problem and not each other, an idea they had learned in Third Option.

Despite Rebecca's changing mind-set about her marriage, she had yet to overcome one roadblock on the road to progress: she still had a hard time trusting Tim. Rebecca realized during the second Third Option course that she had never respected or trusted Tim the way a wife should. At that point, she chose to risk being vulnerable with her husband.

She made herself vulnerable by being honest with Tim, acknowledging his feelings, and giving up her constant ultimatums. As Rebecca let go of her anger and continued to acknowledge her own role in their conflicts, Tim responded by showing his wife greater tenderness and compassion.

The couple also learned that spending quality time with one another was critical to mending their relationship. Spending more time together enabled them to grow together rather than apart. Growing together gave their relationship a renewed vitality and increased their capacity to trust each other.

After the second Third Option course, the Harts knew that the wisdom they had gained from their experience was too important to lose. In an effort to keep the momentum going, they went through the program a third time, and then a fourth. With each Third Option series, they learned more from the mentor couples and more about themselves. They continued working through conflicts and solidifying their commitment to one another.

Today, Rebecca and Tim serve as Third Option mentors, sharing the good news of their saved marriage with other struggling couples. They feel tremendously blessed by the surprising turn of events that eventually led to their healing, both as individuals and as a couple. While their marriage is still a work in progress, Rebecca and Tim agree that it wasn't until they both let go of their anger and allowed God to heal them that things finally began to turn around.

Though it took decades, they feel that the years of unheeded wake-up calls and the challenges of Third Option pushed them slowly toward the eventual transformation of their marriage. Now, the Harts' relationship is richer than they ever could have imagined.

Once inexplicably attracted to Rebecca in middle school, Tim now believes that his match to that bubbly, brown-haired girl was nothing short of divine providence. God brought them together and kept them together through it all. The Harts agree that their saved marriage is miraculous in every way.

—As told to Heather Zydek

The Third Option is a ministry founded on the reality that many couples who are hurting see only two options regarding their situation: enduring a miserable relationship or getting a divorce. The Third Option is an interdenominational marriage education program that seeks to provide couples with another choice: reconciliation.

The Third Option uses workshops and couples' support groups to teach couples the necessary skills to build happier, healthier relationships—to truly reconcile. The ongoing group format can be used to aid in crisis intervention or to enrich any marriage. The Third Option was the 2005 winner of the prestigious Impact Award.

The Third Option
1342 Lancaster Ave.
Syracuse, NY 13210
(315) 472-6728
www.thethirdoption.com
pat@thethirdoption.com

The drug culture isn't something you just decide to leave. It has a way of keeping you trapped. He felt his heart reach out for Rhonda. For once he'd found a woman he couldn't just walk out on.

Kelly sat at the table, straightening the edges of the money so it would fit neatly into the briefcase. Tomorrow he would drive to Redwood City for his wedding, but right now he was more concerned with the 10 kilos of cocaine they were moving from Colombia every week.

Some friends threw darts nearby, while another across the table shifted the customary .44 Magnum to make room for his habit. Groups of people were scattered throughout the dealer's ranch. They came, did a little business, and got wasted. It was all part of the lifestyle.

He knew Rhonda wouldn't want him out so late, but he figured if she didn't like it she could move on. He knew she wouldn't leave, though. She didn't have any friends of her own since she'd moved with him to Carmel. And she was too shy and had too little confidence to leave him. They would fight, and he would walk out if the argument got hot. But she would stay there, watching him go. And she'd always be there when he returned.

So after another night of partying Kelly stumbled out of the car and into the house. At least he hadn't called her to pick him up this time. She hated when he did that. He passed out on the bed, too far gone to notice Rhonda whispering his name.

• • •

Rhonda took a slow, deep breath, attempting to calm her nerves as their small poolside wedding ceremony began. "Memory" from the musical *Cats!* serenaded them from the boom-box with its dismal message. Somehow it was fitting. A drug dealer stood to Kelly's right, a dealer's wife to her left. It was surreal, to say the least.

Holly and Angie looked cute in their little white dresses, smiling up at Mommy. Granted, Holly's eyes seemed a little guarded, but the marriage would give them the security they'd been lacking. Maybe Holly could begin to believe that Kelly would be around for the long haul. Rhonda hoped they could finally unite as a family.

Kelly looked good too, but then he always had. She thought of him all those years ago in Hawaii when she had first seen him. Rhonda had just been divorced for the first time. She'd gone there on vacation with a couple of friends. She'd spotted Kelly and thought he was cute, but it hadn't gone beyond that. And he had been so strung out that he didn't even remember meeting her.

It wasn't until after her second marriage—a huge mistake for which her youngest little girl, Angie, was the only redemption—that she had run into Kelly again. He was in Redwood City, California, hanging out with his friend Mark, who was working on the house Rhonda owned with her mother.

Kelly invited Rhonda to a birthday party they were throwing for his best friend. They began a relationship that night and had been together ever since. Now Kelly was entrenched in the drug scene, and she was lingering in the shadows, isolated. After the move to Carmel, she never went out unless it was to the grocery store. Kelly joked that her best friend was the cashier at Safeway.

Rhonda returned her attention to the wedding. The officiator stood before them, ready to guide them through their vows. *Oh boy, here we go.*

•   •   •

In the days and weeks after the wedding, life in Carmel returned to the usual pattern. Every morning Rhonda would get the girls off to school and then drift through the day in a haze of depression. Every evening Kelly would go to the dealer's house, where he stayed most of the night. Sometimes he made road trips to run money, and he'd had several near run-ins with the law.

Rhonda worried constantly. There was nothing safe about life in the drug world. What would happen to them if he got arrested —or worse? Plus, he was always gone. Sometimes she went with him to the parties. She hated coming home to the rising of the sun and how awful she felt the next day, but in some ways it was better than always being alone. She was far too familiar with that feeling. But even when Kelly was home, the drugs made him difficult to be around.

She sat on the couch, the TV droning in the background. She thought about all the years she had spent alienated and lonely before she'd met Kelly. In her search for love, she had made a lot of bad decisions. She'd been disappointed so many times. She'd been let down repeatedly by men and sex. She couldn't even seem to find love in the house of God.

She had always wanted to be near Jesus, especially during childhood, when her grandmother would talk to her about spiritual things and pray with her. Her parents had insisted that she go to church, but they wouldn't go themselves. Because of her strained relationship with her own father, she had always felt distanced from "God the Father." She pictured Him sitting in heaven with a disapproving frown on His face, pointing His finger at her mistakes. Her earthly father, who had died years ago, hadn't known how to bridge the distance between them. As far as she could tell, he hadn't even tried.

Rhonda sat motionless in her living room, just existing—until the doorbell rang and the mailman handed her a package. Staring at the address, she saw that it was from Kelly's brother, Tony. She opened the box and found a children's story Bible inside.

●   ●   ●

That night, Kelly spotted the Bible laying on the dinner table. He picked it up and thumbed through it. The stories reminded him of his childhood. It seemed natural to begin reading it to the girls, so he did. After that, it became a pretty regular thing when he was home.

Some time after this Kelly needed to create a legitimate front for his drug operation, so he set up a marine and industrial supply company. Kelly was busier than ever. His time with the girls dwindled—not that he had ever spent a lot of time at home. It was one of the things he and Rhonda frequently fought about, and it made it difficult to connect as a family.

Rhonda's oldest daughter, Holly, had learned not to get attached to the men in her mother's life, and Kelly was no exception. Angie, being younger, had welcomed Kelly with open arms. But not Holly. Rhonda and Kelly figured it would take Holly awhile to come around. When they were together, he would play with them and rile them up. Then he would go off to the dealer's ranch.

Eventually Rhonda started working some at the supply business. That way she and Kelly got to occasionally see each other during the day. But she continued insisting that they leave Carmel and the life they were living. When she got pregnant, the situation came to a head.

"Kelly, I want out of here," Rhonda said. "I can't live like this anymore." She turned to look out the glass doors into the peaceful, green valley. When she faced him again, her eyes were determined. "I'm leaving, and I want you to come with me."

Something had been gradually changing in Kelly in the weeks and months leading up to this moment. He remembered the time they had gone to church together and how, from some deep well of remembrance, he had known every word of the Doxology. He thought of how the words of the children's Bible had quietly filled his soul—even through a fog of drugs.

But he was stuck. The drug culture isn't something you just decide to leave. It has a way of keeping you trapped. He felt his heart reach out for Rhonda. For once he'd found a woman he couldn't just walk out on. He knew it wouldn't be easy to walk away from his drug lifestyle, but he couldn't bear the thought of her leaving him behind.

He slowly nodded. "Okay. I don't know how we're going to get out of this, but I'll try."

The opportunity came sooner than he had expected. There were major drug busts happening all over the nation, and many of them were connected to the dealer Kelly worked for in Carmel. The gang began to scatter. And since the dealer owed the cartel millions of dollars, he had bigger fish to fry than Kelly. So he let him go. Kelly and Rhonda packed up the girls and moved back to Redwood City.

Determined to begin everything with a clean slate, they decided to straighten out their finances. During the three years they'd spent in Carmel, they had never filed taxes. Now they did—and found themselves owing huge sums of money. Not only did they owe back taxes, but they owed penalties as well. They knew they couldn't afford to repay this amount any time soon. With no home, no job, a baby on the way, and bank accounts frozen by the IRS, they were in a tough spot.

They moved in with Rhonda's mother while Kelly looked for work. Then one Friday afternoon while they were sitting on the porch, Rhonda's water broke. She was only sixteen weeks along. Frantically, she called her new obstetrician.

"You're probably going to lose this baby," the doctor said casually. "There's nothing you can do." The indifference that met her desperate plea for help was chilling.

Over the weekend, a friend recommended a specialist. When the office opened on Monday, they rushed in. But it was too late. The specialist told them the situation was now dangerous for Rhonda, and there was no chance for the baby. They would have to operate. Hours later, Rhonda woke from general anesthesia, crying. A week later, a nurse called with the autopsy results: she'd lost a perfect baby girl.

It was a breaking point for them. Both Rhonda and Kelly turned to God for comfort. And through the pain of losing what would have been his only biological child, Kelly realized that he already had two children who needed him to start acting like a father.

They started going to church with Kelly's brother, Tony. Rhonda rededicated her life to Christ, and Kelly began to reach for Him. Throughout the next year, Kelly would raise his hand to accept Christ every week — he wanted to be sure he had his bases covered.

Tony steered them toward a couples' Sunday school class. This class had a practice in which one couple would meet with another to have brunch and get to know each other. Kelly and Rhonda went to lunch with Joe and Tammy and hit it off with them right away.

Joe was a church maintenance guy who happened to have a project coming up. Sipping his coffee, he looked Kelly over and nodded once, seeming to make up his mind. "Do you know how to build a fence?"

"I think I could figure it out," Kelly answered, remembering work he had done for the dealer before he had started running money.

Joe smiled. "Then show up tomorrow and we'll find out."

Soon after working with Joe on that job, Kelly was hired by the church as a full-time maintenance worker. He painted apartments on the side. In time, he worked at getting his real estate license.

Their large church community surrounded Kelly and Rhonda with love. They invested time in them and fostered their spiritual growth. One particular woman spent a lot of time with Rhonda, helping her to grasp the truth and grace of God that are "beyond understanding." With the help of this woman, Rhonda finally began to see God as a loving Father.

Kelly began attending a weekly Bible study with the pastors. It was the perfect environment for a novice to learn from mature Christians—and a chance to cut all ties with his past. Before Kelly and Rhonda knew it, they were on the steering committee for the couples' class and were giving of themselves to the church body, as well as receiving the support it had to offer.

Soon, they were able to live on their own again. They moved to a shabby triplex and drove a beat-up old truck that ran only when it felt like it. They didn't have much, but they were happier than they had ever been.

One day the pastor invited Kelly and Rhonda to give their testimony to a crowd of six thousand people at Shoreline Amphitheatre. The shy, self-conscious Rhonda of the past would never have done something like that. But this was a transformed Rhonda. In awe of all God had done for her, she was able to forget herself and remember Him instead. As Kelly stood waiting for his turn to speak, he couldn't take his eyes off his wife. He fell in love with her all over again, amazed at the confident, godly woman she had become.

Life had changed for Kelly too. He recalled his thirtieth birthday, only a year before. A number of his drug dealer "friends" had flown in to attend his party. Now he was turning thirty-one, and God gave him a miracle. For years, Kelly had gone to bed every night wondering where he was going to get the next day's cocaine. When he accepted Christ, the thought went away. Now Kelly understands that sometimes God delivers people *from* their struggle, and sometimes He delivers them *through* their struggle. In his case, God took the craving away. Kelly knew it must be God, because that's not something that "just happens" for addicts. But with God, all things really are possible.

Still, not everything was going smoothly at home. In their early fervor as new Christians, they found comfort not only in the grace of the gospel but also in the newfound guidelines the Bible provided for their lives. Although the obvious change in Kelly and his involvement with the girls had convinced them that he was there to stay, the girls began to resent the couple's new insistence on "following the rules."

"You're not my father!" Holly would yell. "You can't tell me what to do!" How many times had Rhonda heard that lately? Holly began spending more time at her biological dad's home, even living with him off and on.

While God was transforming Rhonda and Kelly's lives, their children were beginning a bumpy ride. The mistakes of Kelly and Rhonda's past still lived on to shadow the children. The exhilaration and joy of their salvation were mixed with the bitterness of watching their daughters experience hurts and rejections. Still, they stood together through the difficulties.

In the process, Rhonda and Kelly reevaluated the types of discipline they'd grown up with. They decided to approach some things differently. Although they were never as lenient as the girls' fathers, they did set aside physical punishment in favor of firm and steady follow-through. They made themselves human and reachable, available and supporting. No matter what problems the girls faced, they ultimately knew where to turn. And somewhere along the way, Kelly became a father to them, even if they never called him by that name.

•   •   •

After nearly twenty years of marriage, Rhonda tried on her new wedding dress. She and Kelly were planning to renew their vows. She turned around in front of the mirror, enjoying the delicacy of the ivory hand-beaded gown. This time, the wedding would be beautiful and filled with hope. The people in attendance would be devoted to God, not addicted to drugs. Their former life could only have destroyed them—individually and as a couple and family. But their journey with Christ had led them closer together.

Everything had turned out so differently than it might have. Soon after committing his life to Christ, Kelly had also truly committed to Rhonda. He had begun treating her with a kind of sacrificial love that considered her needs above even his own. Her natural response had been to treat him the same way—lovingly and respectfully. It had been the beginning of real healing between them. Now Rhonda grinned, overjoyed at the thought: *I am truly marrying my best friend.*

Kelly and Rhonda aren't a perfect couple, and they don't have a perfect family. Sometimes they still struggle with the fact that the girls are still fighting to overcome the hurts of their past. But Rhonda and Kelly love each other and their girls, and their marriage has triumphed over statistics that never would have predicted they would be thriving at year twenty-two.

"Shy" Rhonda is the director of women's ministries at their church. And Kelly has become an elder in the church. He speaks exuberantly of his wife, the "best wife in the world, my best friend," and finds comfort in knowing that she'll always be there with him.

They marvel at the transformation God has wrought in

them — one that could not only nullify the selfishness and neediness of addiction, but that could also reach beyond the grave to heal an uncertain girl's relationship with her father. Rhonda now knows for herself the love her father could not express in life. She is free of that hurt from so long ago.

The joy between Rhonda and Kelly is beyond anything they could have imagined in the harsh, early years. God took a couple on the verge of ruin and redeemed them. He has birthed beauty from ashes.

—As told to Lisa Holloway

Kelly and Rhonda Lawson found very few stepfamily support resources available when they were going through their difficulties in the 1980s. Now, however, there is an abundance of help available from ministries nationwide.

One such ministry is Successful Stepfamilies, founded by Ron Deal. This ministry helps blended families nourish their relationships and cope effectively with the special challenges a stepfamily faces. Ron also travels the nation, presenting the popular seminar, "Building a Successful Stepfamily," at churches throughout the United States. He is also the author of the book *The Smart Stepfamily.*

Successful Stepfamilies
Ron Deal
7905 London Court
Amarillo, TX 79119
(806) 356-7701
www.successfulstepfamilies.com
nan.deal@successfulstepfamilies.com

FRANK *and* JULIE 9

Their relationship simmered and stewed for three years until it finally boiled over. Frank and Julie soon became "married singles," divided by work and the children in their midst.

Frank was living a double life. On the surface, he was doing a decent job of "keeping up appearances." He had a wife, two beautiful young daughters, a nice house, and lots of friends. But inside, his mind was buzzing with paranoia from a long list of lies.

"You'd better not drive that way today—what if someone sees you?"

"Don't park the car there—park around back where no one will see it."

"What is Julie thinking? Is she suspicious?"

The anxiety started taking a toll on his health. He had once been strong and athletic, but now Frank was suffering intense headaches. Though he underwent blood tests, CAT scans, and MRIs, doctors were never able to determine his mystery ailment. Frank eventually attributed the headaches to the stress of hiding his countless lies and secrets. He didn't sleep. He dropped thirty-five pounds. He often wondered if anyone would miss him if he took his life. Surely, he thought, his wife and daughters would be better off with his life insurance than with him.

GROWING SUSPICIONS

Julie started receiving anonymous calls warning her that something was brewing between Frank and one of his co-workers. At first Frank denied any wrongdoing and chastised his wife for her lack of trust. After a second anonymous tip, she called Frank at work and ordered him to come home. He refused, claiming innocence. Someone was setting him up, he said.

Julie didn't know what to believe. So she shifted into detective mode, questioning Frank about his whereabouts, scouring his backpack, checking the caller ID, and calculating the mileage on the car.

One day Frank was gone for hours. Julie called everywhere. No one had seen him. "Where were you?" Julie asked calmly when Frank finally got home.

Frank rattled off all the errands he'd been running.

"No," she said. "I called all those places, and you were never there. Where were you?"

Frank was out of excuses. He had no choice but to admit that he was having an affair.

Julie felt vomit rising in her throat. She was too dizzy to stand.

Julie and Frank separated.

THE SEPARATION

While she and Frank were separated, Julie couldn't escape her feelings of rejection, desperation, and, most of all, rage. The anger would come after she heard that Frank had taken his girlfriend to a volleyball game. It would come when a friend called to say she had just seen Frank and his girlfriend at Sunday Mass. Julie's body burned with fury. She confronted Frank every time, sometimes even chasing him down the street, pounding on his car windows and screaming at him.

"You belong with me, your *wife*! You belong with your *family*, your *little girls*! You *promised* me in front of God and all our friends that we'd be together 'til death do us part'! You're supposed to love *me*!"

THE "OTHER WOMAN"

One evening during their separation it was Frank's night to take care of their two young daughters. When Julie opened the door that day, Frank didn't look well.

"I feel ill," he said. "Could you just keep the girls?"

"Absolutely!" she said. Two points for Julie. She noted in a journal that Frank had been unwilling to watch the kids that night. She wanted to have plenty of documentation to use against him if she needed to.

At bedtime, the girls wanted to call and say goodnight to Daddy. And Julie wanted to confirm Frank's story.

Frank's mother answered the phone. "Frank's not here," she said. "He went to play softball."

Julie's body shook with anger. She put the girls in the car and raced to the ballpark, constructing her plan on the way. She intended to march onto the field, plop the kids down, and scream, *"These children are your responsibility tonight!"*

Julie stomped into the park with one daughter in hand and one on her hip.

Then it hit her.

Frank wasn't there just for softball.

She confronted him, seething. "Where is she?" Frank pointed to the stands. There Julie spotted the "other woman."

Julie stormed over to the woman and took a swing at her. She missed pathetically and dropped her youngest daughter in the process. In a humiliated rage she targeted Frank. People in the crowd jumped up and held her back as she flailed and kicked at her husband. Frank stared blankly at Julie as his mistress attempted to shelter Julie's horrified children.

"Somebody get that woman's hands off my children!" Julie screamed. She picked up her shoe from the gravel, smacked Frank across the temple with the heel, and clawed Frank's neck and face. Bawling and quaking, Julie left with the girls and headed for help from her family and friends.

The next day Julie was arrested in front of her home — someone at the ballpark the night before had called the police. She sobbed the entire time, later calling her mom to bail her out.

But Frank beat her to it. When Julie found out that he had used all of their house payment money to get her out of jail, she was outraged. She couldn't look at Frank. She felt she could never trust or respect him again. Frank went back to their house, and Julie went to live with her mom, where she stayed for a month.

For Frank's part, the situation at the ballpark had been so volatile that he immediately ended his affair and never saw the "other woman" again.

BROKEN PIECES

For the next year, Julie and Frank awkwardly tried to piece together their shattered relationship. But as time passed, it became apparent they were together only for the sake of their children.

It was the financial disaster that came in the wake of Frank's affair that led the couple to the brink of divorce. Julie and the girls went away for the weekend, and while they were gone, a certified letter was delivered, addressed to Julie, informing her that her wages were going to be garnished to repay a debt Frank owed the other woman. Frank threw the letter in the trash, but when Julie returned she found the letter. Julie was sued, paying a second time for Frank's affair. Julie was enraged. She took the letter as a sign from God that the time had come to end the marriage for good.

Julie immediately filed for divorce, and Frank was ordered to vacate their house.

For Julie, divorce definitely seemed to be the way out. Who would put up with years of bitterness and angry words? This isn't love, is it? Love is a feeling. Love can come and go on a whim. Love can be won and lost. And if the feeling goes, love must be dead. A dead relationship is painful. She believed divorce would ease the pain.

In the months leading up to the divorce, Frank began to think that maybe Julie was right—maybe divorce was the answer. All the apologies, all the remorse, all the begging had been met with Julie's cold shoulder. In fact, Julie made sure Frank's life was hell. She would pretend to let him kiss her but instead would bite his lip or spit in his face. She threw the past up at him at every turn.

YOUNG AND IN LOVE

Their early years of young love seemed a million miles away. Then, a younger, happier Frank and Julie had met at a summer cook-out held by a mutual friend. Later that summer, during a party at Julie's house, Frank decided to surprise her in the doorway with a soft, spontaneous kiss. Julie melted.

When the two started dating, Julie felt complete bliss. She loved his strength, his broad smile, and his bold, self-assured demeanor. And Frank couldn't get enough of Julie.

Soon, the young lovers spent all their time together. They would go for a drive or spend the day doing nothing but lying around in each other's arms. They wrote each other long love letters. From the start, they were always on the go, doing something fun together—weekends in nearby Chicago, tennis games, visits to Door County, the Green Bay Packers Hall of Fame. They never needed a plan; they just did what made them happy.

Four years into their relationship Frank gave Julie a box of chocolates on Valentine's Day. Julie was delighted to find an engagement ring inside. On their wedding day, Julie felt proud and confident to have weathered the ups and downs of a long, passionate, four-year courtship. When the big day finally arrived, Julie practically bounded down the aisle.

Early in their marriage, Frank and Julie shared a mutual desire to stay busy and entertained. They went to movies, concerts, and festivals. They had no trouble hopping in the car and driving to Chicago for a day trip. They had two good cars and they always dressed the part when they went out for a nice dinner. They enjoyed great food and good wine. They both worked full-time, and each had a part-time job too, affording them the disposable income to do all the hip and trendy things that were so important to them at the time.

The couple celebrated their first anniversary at the most expensive restaurant in town. Julie had only a few sips of champagne that night . . . because she was already five months pregnant.

The breakdown began after the birth of their second daughter. Their relationship simmered and stewed for three years until it finally boiled over. Frank and Julie soon became "married singles," divided by work and the children in their midst. Julie was always worrying about things around the house. Her focus shifted from going out and having fun with Frank to taking care of the kids, working full-time, and juggling household chores.

Frank was still looking for ways to play. Soon he had taken on three nights of softball and one of golf. He became a partner in a local deli and coached high school volleyball. When he was home,

Julie hounded him about the dishes, the laundry on the floor, and the unmowed lawn.

Frank felt cheated if he was asked to help around the house. "How dare you ask me to help?" he'd say. "Don't you see how hard I work?"

Julie would pound her finger on Frank's chest. "I'm sick of this! Your priorities are so screwed up! I might as well be a single parent! Everything in your life comes before me and the girls!"

The things that had first attracted Julie to Frank were now driving her crazy. He was still strong, athletic, and bold. But now being bold meant that he was bold enough to tell her he was adding one night of golf on top of the three nights he already dedicated to softball. Julie begged him to back off, pleading with him that she needed more help at home.

After a late night out, Frank would often crawl into bed eager for sex. Julie would be asleep—or at least pretending to be asleep. Frank was persistent. But Julie didn't think Frank deserved sex. She'd flinch or swat his hands away, hoping to emphasize how exhausted she was from working and entertaining two little ones all day.

Frank saw Julie's disgust in him and his lack of responsibility, so he stayed away.

When Frank took an off-shift job working twelve-hour night shifts, things only got worse. He and Julie rarely saw one another, except when Julie would come home for lunch or when they passed each other at the front door on their way to and from work.

Money was always a concern. They always seemed to be out of money before they were out of month.

As Frank's disillusionment with the relationship grew, he began to look elsewhere for enjoyment. His long hours at work grew longer as he and his co-workers stopped for breakfast at a tavern on the way home. Playing softball on the company team allowed him even more time away.

One woman in particular always seemed to be at the games to watch Frank play, talking to him afterward. Soon, Frank's relationship with his co-worker became physical, turning into a nine-month affair.

ONE MORE CHANCE

With their divorce only five weeks away, Frank clung to one last hope. He hoped that bringing Julie to Retrouvaille, a program designed to help couples heal and renew their marriages, would somehow save their relationship. He was adamant that he and Julie spend the weekend of their sixth anniversary there. Frank's insistence finally swayed Julie to play along, if only for one last weekend.

Before the weekend, Julie felt only anger and contempt for her soon-to-be ex-husband. She tried as hard as she could to remain tough and cold. But inside, she wondered if God had her just where he wanted her: broken down and completely vulnerable. God, she felt, was the only one who knew her secret wish to have her happy family restored.

Neither Julie nor Frank were prepared for the power of their Retrouvaille weekend. Julie sat in awe and cried as she listened to other couples onstage. As part of the weekend they had to write letters to one another. Frank's dialogue letters, Julie felt, were like an open book straight into his head and his heart. With each dialogue, Julie's perception of Frank changed. This was the man she knew and loved after all.

Throughout the weekend, Frank remembered the joy of their wedding day and the vows they had made to one another, something that helped him begin to put into perspective just how much damage he had done. Learning that marriage partners can make daily decisions to forgive and commit to their spouses helped Frank to move forward in his marriage. Understanding that love is an action, a clear and conscious decision, not a feeling, helped Frank and Julie to see just how possible it was to smooth things out.

Presentation after presentation, dialogue after dialogue, Frank and Julie were bowled over with an entirely new perspective on their marriage. The stories of their Retrouvaille weekend presenters, other couples who had weathered rough patches in their own marriages, gave Frank and Julie hope. Julie realized she might actually be capable of loving Frank by changing her own negative attitude. Maybe the pain-filled year after the affair was really a gift from God: the gift of time. Time to grieve. Time to process all the mixed-up emotions inside.

Frank was overwhelmed when he learned on Saturday night that Julie was ready to forgive him. The feeling of cleansing was like a shower after a long day out in the dirt, watching the thick blackness wash away. For Frank, that dirt was guilt and shame—it all washed away as he fell asleep in Julie's arms that night. *This is going to be a way of life,* he thought. He told the presenting couples on his way out the door on Sunday that he and Julie would one day be sharing their own story with other struggling couples.

Frank and Julie LaBoda knew the road ahead would be long and hard, so they continued attending Retrouvaille's post-sessions. Today, they still cling to the lifeline of Retrouvaille. They rely on the support of other couples on the same journey: continuing to better their marriage relationships.

Retrouvaille's emphasis on dialogue brought new life to the LaBodas' nearly dead marriage. After their weekend they decided to live from this day forward. There was nothing they could do about the past, but they could affect the future. Each day they could decide to commit, love, trust, and forgive one another.

Frank and Julie found an exit ramp off the road to divorce. Through Retrouvaille and God's unconditional love, and the support of Retrouvaille, they experienced incredible feelings of hope and wonder, like making a wrong turn only to discover a beautiful place they never expected to find.

—*Frank and Julie Laboda (with Heather Zydek)*

∞•∞

Frank and Julie Laboda are currently serving as the international coordinators of Retrouvaille. *Retrouvaille* is a French word meaning "rediscovery"—and that's just what this program is about.

During Retrouvaille weekends and follow-up, emphasis is given to rediscovering each other through special techniques of communication. These techniques enable the couple to explore most areas of the relationship respectfully and constructively in a private setting. Retrouvaille has helped thousands of couples in cold or broken relationships find healing and renewal; it is available in multiple locations throughout the United States and Canada and in twenty-one countries worldwide.

Retrouvaille
(800) 470-2230
www.retrouvaille.org

*"The cry of the heart is for intimate connection with yourself,
with others, and with God— whom I never believed could
love or care for a 'whore' like me."*

The great Western novelist Louis L'Amour opens his novel *Lonely on the Mountain* with this line: "There will come a time when you believe everything is over. That will be the beginning." As a writer, when I first read L'Amour's line I thought it was a wonderful way to begin a book. Today, on a much deeper level, I understand what those words really mean.

The "over" state in my life and marriage came in the winter of 1990, when I received the devastating diagnosis of early stage cervical cancer caused by the sexually transmitted disease HPV (human papillomavirus). As I hung up the phone after the doctor's call, my mind raced with images of medical treatments, of figuring out how to care for my young children while I was ill, and especially of telling my husband.

I knew that my secret life was about to be exposed.

David and I had married in 1981 (just a few weeks after the wedding of Prince Charles and Princess Diana), and for the first few years we had been very happy. It was a second marriage for us both, but we'd each married young, neither of us had any children, and we both had divorced after only four years. We viewed our life together as an opportunity to start over after a serious misstep in our youth. David had an excellent position in a Fortune 100 company, and we had more money than we needed to be comfortable. Within a few years we were blessed with a beautiful, healthy young daughter and son.

But underneath the veneer of tranquil, suburban, upper-middle-class life, I harbored a number of secrets. The darkest one—and the one most pertinent to my health issue—was a secret I'd successfully hidden for almost twenty years . . . something I had denied, rationalized, and justified since the age of fourteen . . . a reality too painful to admit and so rare in women that I'd never heard its name: *I was a sex addict.*

At the time of my cervical cancer diagnosis, I was intensely involved in an extramarital affair. It was only the latest of many similar relationships throughout both my marriages. In fact, my unfaithfulness had been the reason for the end of my first marriage.

It was two more years before I heard that clinical diagnosis of sexual addiction, and even then, it was almost impossible to accept. A sex addict? What a horrible name! Surely that description didn't apply to me. I was a nice, conservative, churchgoing soccer mom with a college degree and a long list of accomplishments. I had an equally nice husband, though I'd come to quietly resent him over the years.

David worked hard and provided well. He was a kind, gentle man with a methodical head on his shoulders and a calm demeanor. He had a giving spirit and was a good father. He, however, was unfamiliar with the landscape of intimacy. David was a practical man, not an emotional one. He didn't know how to talk about matters of the heart, and he wasn't able to show his feelings.

Though I'd initially been attracted to his stability, I'd come to resent his lack of spontaneity and emotional presence. I viewed him as boring, shutdown, and worse. I blamed him for the growing detachment in our marriage and for my growing discontent. I wondered how I'd again married the wrong person, and I believed that if I were married to Mr. Right, my life would be the magical one I had always dreamed of.

EARLY ON . . .

I had little understanding of my own behavior and less understanding of my own story. I was a preacher's daughter who had been raised in the church. Our family looked perfect and was widely respected. I was raised with many advantages and was an excellent, popular student. Sure, we'd had our share of sorrow. When I was three years old, my mother had died from colon cancer, and my two older brothers and I were left to be raised largely by a grandmotherly helper who came to live in our home.

Our family spiritualized our feelings of grief, and we never talked about our loss. My father, brothers, and I soldiered on, each lost in our separate pain. My father buried himself in "God's work" and gave little time to his family, which was the custom for his generation, especially for members of the clergy. As a grown woman with children of my own, I had no idea how deeply I had been impacted by my mother's death and my father's absence.

I had even less understanding of the rest of my story. Like most people, I viewed my situation as normal. Beginning when I was five years old, a dear family friend assumed a fatherly role in my life, and for the next fifteen years he was a central figure in our home. It was a very positive relationship in many ways as he taught me how to roller skate, encouraged me as a fledgling writer, and listened to my hopes and dreams.

However, this friend also exposed me to lots of pornography (and himself), and he steadily groomed me as a sexual predator. In gradually escalating sexual activity, he exploited my loneliness, which he filled with fun activities during the day and long talks deep into the night when my father was away. I was ten years old before I realized that some of the things we were doing must be "sex," which, of course, was never discussed in my home. By the time we actually had intercourse when I was fourteen, the only way I could make sense of the sexual relationship was to blame myself.

My friend was gentle and "loving" with me. He spent time with me and was attentive to me. I loved him and sought his company. He said he loved me and that our relationship was special. How could I not be at fault for our sexual activity? I believed I had chosen (as a ten-year-old!) to be sexual with a man fifteen years my senior. Especially by the time I was fourteen and running my family's household, I thought I was old enough to choose to have sex with a man almost old enough to be my father.

And when I kept choosing to have sex as a promiscuous teen (desperate for the love and attention this man had removed), there was only one way I could frame my behavior: *I was a whore*, a horrible, terrible person. That identity was my internal self-description for the next twenty years, and I lived it out in a variety of ways.

I never told a soul about my double life, and I protected my secret with overachievement and perfection. I followed my father and brothers in pouring myself into church work. At the same time, I medicated my loneliness and shame with relationships that were both intense and sexual.

I thought that getting married would cure my promiscuity. Soon, though, I discovered my husband couldn't fill the gaping, black hole inside, which I could only identify as an aching, tender place within. Eventually, I resumed my pattern of looking for love in the arms of men. With each affair, I shrouded my heart in another blanket of shame. I knew my behavior was wrong, but I was powerless to stop despite my many attempts. At that point I had no clue that what I was doing fit the classic definition of an addiction.

FACING THE TRUTH

My diagnosis of cervical cancer caused by a sexually transmitted disease was God's wake-up call on my life. I was forced to confirm for David the affairs he had long suspected and chosen to ignore. The diagnosis propelled us onto a path we had never dreamed we would walk, a path that today we view with immense gratitude.

At first we focused on my physical healing, and I went through three surgeries in the next twelve months. Eventually, the cancer was gone and my body healed. But I discovered my spirit and soul were still diseased.

Despite my good intentions, I continued in my latest affair. I knew my behavior (including unprotected sex) was literally killing me, but I was powerless to stop. Finally, with desperate thoughts of suicide bouncing darkly behind my eyes, I did something I had never done before: *I asked for help.* I called a dear friend, poured out my truth, and received grace that was shocking and amazing. I began an intense period of therapy, and the healing began.

With the help of a gifted Christian counselor, I came to understand my story. I put the responsibility for my early sexual activity back on the abuser, which is where it belonged. I grieved the abandonment from my mother and also my father, and I saw that my affairs were just false solutions to deep inner pain and legitimate needs. Eventually, I let others into my life when I became active in a twelve-step group for recovery from sexual addiction. With the help of safe, intimate friends, I was able to end unsafe, sinful affairs. I learned what genuine intimacy felt like, and to my surprise, it wasn't sexual.

I learned that sexual addiction really isn't about sex at all, which is something I had intuitively always known. It is an *intimacy disorder*—a desperate search for love, touch, affirmation, affection, and approval. Obviously, sexual addiction is false intimacy and a false solution for legitimate needs, but it's driven by pain and loneliness, not by physical gratification. The cry of the heart is for intimate connection with yourself, with others, and with God— whom I never believed could love or care for a "whore" like me.

The best part of the healing process was coming to know a God I'd never imagined, a God of pursuing grace who was fully able to meet my needs. I traded my rules-based religion for relationship-based spirituality. (Grace motivates in a way that shame cannot, and I longed to respond to God's love with obedience rather than perform out of fear.) In every way, I became a "new creature."

DAVID'S PAST

Obviously, my marriage improved when I remained faithful to it. But David and I discovered after a few years that our healing journey was still significantly incomplete. Though David looked liked the much healthier one in our coupleship (after all, he hadn't had affairs or done the terrible things I had), our counselor gently identified his own areas of impairment. We realized David had his own demons to deal with, especially in the area of his profound, untreated depression, which crippled and isolated him.

He too was raised in a clergyman's family, though his upbringing was significantly healthier than mine. David was spared sexual abuse and other forms of recognizable trauma. He had loving parents and a brother who all were positive figures in his life.

But David's internal landscape was shaped in ways just as profound as mine. When he was a young child, his father had an extended hospitalization for catatonic depression, which in the dark days of mental health treatment in the 1950s was just as shameful as sex addiction is today. His family was embarrassed, and they too never talked about their experience.

During their dad's hospitalization, David's brother went to

live with family members three hundred miles away, because his hyperactivity was too much for their stressed mother to handle. (No one knew of ADHD in the 1950s, either.) David learned the best way to navigate life was to be quiet, avoid attention or conflict, ignore his own needs, and wait for the hard times to pass. He too struggled with an intimacy disorder—which was actually just the other side of the coin from mine.

HEALING AND A FRESH START

Unknowingly, David and I were two wounded people who had each found another wounded person to dovetail with our pain. For each of us, the greatest (unrecognized) fear was abandonment, and we unconsciously believed we had found someone who would never leave us as the key figures of our childhood had. In David's stability, I thought I'd found security, and in my dominant personality, he thought he'd found someone resilient and strong like his mother. Sadly, we both were wrong.

Yet God gave our marriage a new beginning, one that didn't come until we thought the marriage was over. We were surprised to discover God had an amazing plan for our coupleship. From our deepest wounds, including the ones we'd inflicted on each other, our heavenly Father forged our deepest healing.

After two and a half years of my sobriety from sexual addiction and significant healing from core trauma, we took a second major turn in the road when David embraced his own healing journey. He began to explore his story and how it had shaped the man he had become. He discovered crucial things about himself that had impacted our relationship, and he bravely addressed them. He did so in his sweet, methodical fashion, which by this point I had come to appreciate.

David learned how to identify his feelings and fears and how to share them with me, which was harder for him. He risked stating his needs and engaging in healthy conflict. He did his own recovery work, including taking part in a twelve-step program for co-sex addiction. He stepped up to the plate and assumed responsibility for his part in our relationship dance.

Slowly we learned what it meant to be a genuinely intimate couple. We became emotional and spiritual partners instead of just practical cohorts. The roots of our coupleship grew deeper and our bond stronger.

I discovered that dear, practical David, who for years had felt emotionally unavailable to me, was actually the one man in my life who had not abandoned me. And David found that despite the deep ways I had betrayed him, I was deeply committed to him and accepted him exactly as he was. We encouraged each other to develop into our healthy, true selves. We found that we greatly complemented each other's strengths and compensated for each other's weaknesses. Together, we became something neither of us could be alone.

Our journeys, separate and together, have moved past our personal lives and have evolved into ministry. At that "over" point of coming to the end of myself, I thought God was through with me. How could I ever do anything positive for God after the profound ways I had failed Him? In this area too I was graced with a new beginning.

A MINISTRY IS BORN

After a year or two of coffee cup counseling, where I talked informally with other women who had similar stories, I returned to graduate school and got a master's degree to counsel professionally. Quickly, my practice centered on sexual addiction and sexual trauma. Before long I came to direct a Christ-centered, therapeutic workshop program for those affected by sexual addiction.

Bethesda Workshops now serve clients from across the country who come to Nashville for help and hope. In this effort too David and I are a meaningful team. I'm the front person, the one visible and in charge, but David is a steady contributing force. He hauls materials to the workshop site and helps with anything behind the scenes that needs doing. He keeps the home fires burning when I'm gone for workshops or speaking engagements, and he supports me when I'm tired or discouraged. When we started affirming each other's natural gifts, we discovered how much we needed each other—and how fulfilling and fun it is to enhance each other.

A few years ago another tragedy provided a measuring stick of how far we had come since our end and our new beginning. We were stunned when David was diagnosed with renal cell carcinoma—advanced kidney cancer. His prognosis was bleak.

One night we were rocking quietly in our darkened den, and David pulled me into his lap and held me close. "I want you to know that no matter what happens, it'll be okay," he promised. "I'm at peace with this situation, and I have no regrets. I'm grateful that we've had such a good life."

I looked at him incredulously. "A *good life*? Now I know you're really sick," I teased. "Where were you during all those awful years? How can you say we've had a good life together?"

David was quiet a few seconds and then responded in his typical understated way. "Yeah, we've had some hard times, I guess. But it took those tough times to get us where we are tonight, and I wouldn't trade being here for anything."

At that moment, I knew the outcome had been worth all the pain of the journey. L'Amour's promise was true: at the time you think everything is over, that will be the beginning.

—*Marnie Feree*

Marnie Feree entered uncharted territory in 1997, establishing a series of workshops for female sex addicts. This was hailed as groundbreaking program, the first of its kind.

Marnie now serves as the director of Bethesda Workshops in Nashville, TN where she resides with her husband, David.

Bethesda Workshops exist as a beacon of hope to anyone, male or female, seeking healing from various forms of sexual addiction ranging from pornography to affairs. Although the workshops are taught from a nondenominational, faith-based approach, participants from all religious affiliations are welcome. Workshops are available for clinicians, medical professionals, and pastors as well as for sex addicts and their spouses/ex-spouses.

Bethesda Workshops
Marnie C. Ferree, MA, LMFT
3710 Franklin Road
Nashville, TN 37204
Toll free (866) 464-HEAL
www.bethesdaworkshops.org
nhobson@bethesdaworkshops.org

Sue tried to train herself to have loving thoughts toward Tom.
But instead, she found a root of resentment growing inside
her heart as she replayed all the ways he had let her down.

When Tom got out of the truck at work, ready to load it for transport, he didn't know what to expect. What was Sue doing here? He hadn't seen her in months — not since she'd moved in with Steve and then left Steve to live with her mother. What now?

Pain registered anew as he watched her open the car door and begin walking toward him. She absentmindedly rested the soft palm of her hand against the roundness of a belly beginning to swell with life. He had heard about the pregnancy, but he didn't know quite how to feel about her. Angry? Hurt? He missed her, but was there really any hope for them — after *this*? After the ways he'd wounded her over the years?

Sue's tension was evident. Even so, there was a glow about her. Tom loved their two grown children, but babies had always lit Sue up in a way he couldn't quite understand. She had always wanted another child. It was almost as if children gave her a place to open her heart and give all the love that other people had rejected in so many ways.

Tom's mouth quirked into a lopsided grin. When their first child was born, he had been in a completely different place in life, passing out celebratory joints to the guys at work. Getting high.

Drinking. Women. They were all quick fixes meant to dull the pain of a depression he couldn't shake in the midst of problems he couldn't define or fix.

"Can we talk?" Sue asked him nervously.

Tom felt his stomach unknot as some of the anxiety left him. "I have to work right now. Meet me for dinner?"

"Okay."

Tom made his way through the rest of the day in a haze as his mind constantly drifted back to the past—the arguments, the counseling, the days spent lying on the black sofa in that depressing gold room, nights spent escaping his family. He also remembered Sue's moodiness, moping, and resentment, and her need to talk about problems he didn't understand.

He had eventually been diagnosed with clinical depression. The antidepressants lifted some of that haze and made him able to see their situation more clearly. He began to change, but it had been too late.

He remembered with sadness the night of their twentieth anniversary—one that should have been a celebration for two people who had just spent half their lives together. But three weeks before that night, Sue had insisted he move out, helping him settle into a little cabin in a nearby town in an effort to relieve some of her guilt. He had never thought it would be permanent. That night he could see the sadness in her eyes over the death of a marriage she had held in her dreams for so long, and it gave him faith there was still a chance. So on the night of their twentieth anniversary he had invited her to his place for dinner, and she had come.

After dinner, they took a walk around the lake. Starlight shimmered on peaceful water as they strolled along the bank. But what should have been a romantic evening took a wicked turn when an argument broke out. Sue had become exasperated with Tom because he didn't seem to understand the magnitude of their ongoing problems. She had grown so frustrated that she'd screamed out her anger, *willing* him to finally get it: "I hate you! I've hated you for years." She shook with rage and rushed away, leaving Tom to stand alone in the shadows.

TWENTY YEARS EARLIER . . .

Sue looked down at the swirling waters pulling at her legs, inviting her to let the river's currents sweep her away and bury her beneath their depths. She'd been flirting with its edge for so many years now that she could almost hear its voice urging her to let it stop the pain.

If she did, she wouldn't have to lose anyone else. It wouldn't matter that nothing she had was really her own to keep forever. That Dad drank too much. That she wasn't special. Still, she resisted the deep, swirling center that called to her. It would have to wait.

Later that night, she showed a different face, wild and free, cruising around town in Jim's convertible. Her sister, Pat, was snuggled up to Jim in the front. Sue sat in back next to Jim's friend, Tom, feeling the wind in her hair. She liked the look of Tom—brown and muscular, masculine and exciting. And he really listened to what she had to say.

Tom liked her too. He thought of her as a real free spirit. She didn't seem afraid of anything. Just tell her she couldn't do something, and she would do it. It was so different from being around his own family, which was completely predictable and kind of distant. Sue's presence was immediate and alive. Tom was tired of living his life in park, and time with Sue was anything but dull.

The attraction was instant, physically and emotionally. Two months later Pat and Jim announced they were getting married. When they did, Sue and Tom decided to go along for the ride and get married too. It seemed like a good idea at the time. And love is always nice, right?

But less than a year into the marriage, their relationship had changed. One night Sue left a party, tears streaming down her face, and waited in the car for Tom. She waited a long time, unwilling to believe the rumors: *He's in that room with his ex-girlfriend,* they'd said. The last time Sue had seen Tom, he'd been hanging out with the guys in some corner. She didn't want to believe what her friends were telling her, though she knew it was probably true.

Tom came out awhile later, looking relaxed as he tossed away an empty beer can. He got in the car without a word and drove away. Sue tried to make herself believe the warm female scent clinging to his skin was just her imagination. She was good at ignoring things she didn't want to think about. After all, her whole life had trained her to bury the pain in a place where no one had to look at it.

I want a baby. The thought took her by surprise, but she knew she needed someone she could love without fear. They postponed it for a while, but eventually she got her wish.

Three and a half years later they had a daughter, and then later a son. Sue hoped that having children would bring back the intimacy she and Tom had shared before the wedding.

But to Tom, Sue was no longer an adventure, the free spirit he had sought outside his own home. Now she had become part of the "home" he'd always tried to get away from. Having children was the beginning of a near-endless round of quick fixes meant to make them okay or provide some other focus besides the pain and disappointment they were feeling.

The hurt Sue felt in her heart began to manifest itself physically: migraines knocked her flat for a week or two at a time. Years passed, moments heaped upon moments of distance and dissatisfaction. Tom knew something was wrong; he just didn't know what. This wasn't *Ozzie and Harriet.* This certainly wasn't the free, wild life he had pictured when he had struck out on his own. There was something missing.

Every afternoon he would somehow drag himself out of bed to go to work. In the evenings, he lived to anesthetize himself: a few drinks, a little partying, detours to strip clubs, and occasional sexual encounters. It never fixed anything, but it made him forget the depression for a little while. It was familiar, "fun," and something to do besides face the fact that he and Sue were a failure.

Sue, on the other hand, had seen in her children's births the chance to start fresh. And she had begun to feel God tugging at her heart. Her desire to have God in her life had grown along with the children as they crawled, walked, spoke their first words, and blew out their birthday candles. This was where they belonged. She wanted them to grow up talking to God and knowing Him in a personal way.

Every week she stifled her annoyance at Tom, who would sit at home getting high and reading the paper. Every day she tried to train herself to have loving thoughts toward him, to focus on becoming a good wife. She had placed the Proverbs 31 tribute to the "wife of noble character" inside the bathroom cabinet to read daily, reminding her of the person she wished she could be.

Instead, she found a root of resentment growing inside her heart as she replayed all the ways Tom had let her down, the holidays he had ruined with his selfishness, the nights she had spent lonely while he partied—the embarrassment she felt when someone would tell her where Tom had been or whom he had been with. She didn't know what to do about those things. The migraines kept her from working regularly, and she had two beautiful little children depending on her. Feeling there was no other choice, she endured the humiliation. *Why hasn't God fixed us yet?* She sank into depression, once again longing for the sweet release of death.

Her prayer life soon faltered along with her faith, and she asked the children to stop praying for her. She was certain now that she would end up keeping the migraines but losing Tom. *I can't love him too much,* she told herself. *If I love him, I will lose him, just like everything else.*

Tom too began reaching to fill the void inside. He eventually accepted the salvation Jesus offered, but he didn't immediately see the outcome he was looking for. He wondered why things didn't suddenly improve, and he grew discouraged. Marriage counseling didn't work, either.

Twenty Years Later

After twenty years together, they separated. They split and reunited several times over a six-year period. Sue began drinking. Tom would meet her for drinks and dancing, thinking it would make her want to be with him. But nothing helped.

Finally, the children graduated and left home for lives of their own, and the thin thread holding them together snapped. The children had been the reason they had used for trying to stay together, and now that reason was gone.

Sue was ready to make a life for herself without the pain of the past—pain she blamed almost entirely on Tom. When she remembered their walk around the lake, their first real breakup, she shook her head, thinking what a miracle of self-control had been required to keep her from pushing him over the steep bank into the water and running away. How wonderful it would be to escape the years of hurt, loneliness, and bitter feelings that had left her heart hard and cold. No, there would be no more reconciliation.

Sue was done with marriage. She thought it was terrible, actually. When a friend announced her own marriage, Sue sent her a sympathy card instead of congratulations. In a step toward self-sufficiency, she found a job and an apartment and brought home a kitten to keep her company. She stopped the drinking that had become her companion over the last several years and started going to twelve-step meetings. She started praying again and taking responsibility for her life.

Soon she moved in with Steve, a man she liked and respected, to keep company with as well. Life was looking up. She finally had some peace. And in time, Steve agreed to have a child with her.

Sue was ecstatic when she found out she was pregnant. Steve sat beside her as they waited during her first obstetrical visit. The doctor sat facing them, looking at her forty-something patient sternly. "We have to know right now if you're going to terminate it. Was this pregnancy planned?"

Simultaneously, she answered, "Yes," and he answered, "No." She was floored by his response. Hadn't he agreed to having a baby together?

From that point on, Steve wanted nothing to do with their child. It was the beginning of the end. Not long after the doctor's visit, Sue found herself lost in thought, sitting atop her washing machine. As she began thinking about all the things that had begun to go wrong, visions of Tom flashed through her mind. She replayed their moments together, good and bad, like something out of a movie. The pictures wouldn't leave her. They came into her mind in the most unpredictable places and visited her in her dreams.

Could it be they were meant to be together after all? *God, no!* But the pictures kept coming.

TOM'S STORY

Tom's journey was different. For a while, he looked for ways to get back together with Sue. But he finally came to sense that God was telling him it was time to let go of her and to get back to church. He dove into a Bible study.

It was there that he met Shelly, who thought he was pretty special—special enough to marry. In an attempt to be fair to her, he moved his separation with Sue to the next level and filed divorce papers. But God would not let go of his heart. In the end, Tom had to be honest with Shelly. He couldn't divorce Sue. She was his wife, no matter what, and it was time to end this new relationship.

Soon after, he was browsing through magazines in the church library, and he saw an ad for a ministry called Covenant Keepers. He tracked down the ministry and began learning what it meant to stand for his marriage. He learned that in the "rope" of each marriage there are three strands: the husband, the wife, and the Holy Spirit—the Helper God has sent to His people on earth. As long as even one human partner in the marriage was willing to hold firm to what was promised in covenant, the Holy Spirit also held firm, and there was still a marriage. There was still hope.

Tom found that Covenant Keepers particularly specializes in working with only one spouse who is trying to keep the marriage in covenant, saving it for the legacy of generations to come. Tom was devastated when he found out about Sue's pregnancy, but he immersed himself deeper into the wisdom and community of Covenant Keepers. Eventually, he found the grace to pray for Sue and for the baby, whom he began loving simply because she was a part of Sue—who was part of him.

Only later did he find out that Covenant Keepers doesn't put ads in magazines.

SUE'S STORY

God had been working on Sue too.

The anxiety kept coming back as Sue pondered her upcoming night with Tom. She shook her arms, trying to work out the tension while she wondered all over again how she had managed the courage to track him down on the job, especially as she sported her brand-new maternity top. She had left Steve and was now living with her mother, and her mom had given her that extra nudge. Her mom had been having conversations of her own with Tom, and she began encouraging Sue to seek him out.

But what will I say to him?

She was still wondering that as she got in the car with him later to go to dinner. They rode in relative silence until the words found her, surprising them both.

"I'm sorry."

She hadn't meant to say it, yet she knew in her heart the words were real.

"Thanks," Tom said. "I've needed to hear that."

They talked for hours, in the car and over dinner, feeling more connected than ever before.

Later Tom paused, wondering if it was too soon to say what was in his heart. After all, they had been split up for five years and hadn't spoken in months. But there was no time to waste.

"I love you, Sue. I want you back, and I want this baby too. I want her to be *our* baby. But I'm moving next week."

Tears shone in Sue's eyes, and she reached for his hand. "If you're going, then I'm going too."

Suddenly, the past didn't matter, and the walls built up inside her came crumbling down. Never before had she felt the love of the Savior so completely. She didn't quite know if she trusted Tom, but she did trust God, who had steadily worked this transformation in them both. The pain Tom had caused her over the years melted away, ceasing to exist. Love and admiration for each other began to replace the bad memories in that moment when God saved their marriage.

STARTING OVER

Tom and Sue slowly built back their relationship, participating regularly with the Covenant Keepers community—this time *together*, shining a light for other damaged couples. In time, Sue gave birth to that little girl, and they named her Morgan. They are often told she looks "just like her daddy." They simply smile and say, "God is good"—a goodness they've come to know ever more deeply as Morgan has grown and filled their house with her sweet, gentle spirit.

Eleven years after their reconciliation, they are still together, still enthralled by the second chance God has given them and by the delight of a young girl who runs to greet her father with the joy of one who knows that she is loved beyond question. Of course, there are still bumps in the road. Every marriage has them. But their love and God's grace are more powerful than any problems. The cycle of broken promises has been shattered, and instead they are leaving behind a legacy of covenant to warm the generations to come.

—As told to Lisa Holloway

∞•∞

Tom and Sue Tegtmeier found help for their hopeless marriage through the Covenant Keepers community, founded by Marilyn Conrad. Covenant Keepers offers support for spouses seeking marital reconciliation. However, it is somewhat unique in that the ministry will work with one spouse, even when the other spouse does not initially want to reconcile.

Over and over, Covenant Keepers has shown that when even one spouse is willing to "stand" for his or her marriage, healing can take place and God can breathe new life into the marriage.

Covenant Keepers operates groups throughout the United States and six other countries.

Covenant Keepers (U.S.)
3434 South Garnett Road, Suite One
Tulsa, OK 74146-2149
 (918) 743-0365
www.covenantkeepersinc.org
info@covenantkeepersinc.org

"Found out." The words pounded over and over through her brain as she numbly hung up the phone. Now she stood in the shadowed doorway, grappling for the strength to stand before Bob and betray her secret and her marriage along with it.

Cathy closed her children's bedroom door, gripping the knob as she struggled to control her breathing. The sudden silence of the house assaulted her senses, thickening in her lungs, roaring to the fevered rhythm of her pulse. This was it.

Padding noiselessly down the hall, she lingered in the doorway, her stomach icy with terror.

Turn around! her mind shrieked. *Just turn around and walk away! You don't have to tell him. Not tonight, not ever . . .*

She froze, her knuckles white on the doorframe, wracked by her indecision. She could hear Bob in the other room, and his unsuspecting presence sickened her with dread. It would be so easy to walk the other way, to go into the bedroom and close the door and pretend that everything was fine. She was a Christian now — had Christ not forgiven her this sin? Why, then, must she do this?

Cathy dug her fingernails into her palms, her wedding ring biting into her flesh. She knew why she had to do this. She could still hear her pastors' voices filling the receiver, urging her to confess. Cathy had called them in a panic as soon as she'd hung up with Jay. She'd poured out the entire story to them, choking on her shame, desperate for a solution. Their advice had been simple, direct, and the one thing she absolutely didn't want to hear: "Cathy, you must tell Bob before he hears it from somebody else."

Immediately her mind had rebelled against their advice. The thought of standing before her husband and telling him about Jay was too terrifying to contemplate. Yet even as she tried to maneuver around the idea, Cathy knew she had no other option. Her secret was out, and it was only a matter of time before Bob heard the truth.

Pressing her damp palm to her cheek, Cathy asked herself yet again what had brought her to this moment, to this place where even the idea of confronting her husband could set her stomach heaving with fear. Things had become so tangled somehow, her marriage twisted into something unrecognizable from the life they had once shared together.

The night she had first met Bob suddenly flared up in her mind.

Looking Back

They had both been just kids then, high school freshmen who had met by coincidence at a school dance. What began as a mutual attraction quickly developed into something deeper. They had dated through high school, their relationship ending and resuming repeatedly during the years that Bob had attended the State University of New York. Unlike the teenaged commitments of their peers, which faded with time, Bob and Cathy's bond endured the distance between them, and they were married shortly after Bob graduated from college.

That day when Cathy had spoken vows of better or worse before the altar, she'd had no idea of the magnitude and speed with which "worse" would descend. A few months after their one-year wedding anniversary, Bob discovered his father in his car, dead from carbon monoxide poisoning. Two days later, Bob was informed of his pending draft notice for the army, with potential service in Vietnam. This news arrived within hours of Cathy's discovery that she was pregnant.

As it turned out, Bob was spared the horrors of the war overseas. To the couples' amazement, God created a vacancy in a local National Guard unit, where there had not been one previously, and he was able to serve there. But not everything worked out so well. Cathy soon began hemorrhaging and later miscarried.

In spite of the hardships, the couple pressed on. They each took refuge in the solace that only the other could provide, bound together perhaps even more tightly by the tragedies they shared. As the days rolled on they stepped carefully forward, carrying the hope of better times like a light between them.

However, the true test of their relationship had hardly begun. During their fifth year of marriage, Bob enrolled with a paramedic squad. One night he rode along on ambulance detail as they rushed to the aid of a choking woman. Upon arriving at the scene, he was appalled to discover that the woman was not a stranger to him but was Cathy's very best friend, Marlene. Despite their best efforts, the team was unable to resuscitate her, and she passed away before Bob's eyes. Numb with anguish, Bob had little choice but to go home and deliver the news to Cathy.

Grief infiltrated their lives like a famine, filling them with the aching void of someone lost who can never be returned. Unlike their previous hardships, Marlene's death twisted their hearts individually, making them unrecognizable to each other in their sorrow.

Bob, who had witnessed the tragedy firsthand, wanted nothing more than to block the terrible images from his mind. Anxious to escape, he turned inward, refusing to talk about the events that surrounded the death or his feelings on the subject. Cathy, on the other hand, was being torn apart from the inside out. Only by talking about the incident did she feel she could move on, as if words could transform Marlene's incomprehensible death into some semblance of sense. The more Cathy tried to talk to Bob about Marlene, the more Bob turned away from her.

Bereaved of her best friend and barred from the solace of her husband, Cathy found herself crushed beneath the weight of her own loneliness. Stricken with anxiety attacks and sinking into depression, she turned increasingly to prescription drugs and alcohol to numb the misery she felt.

In such a condition she was unprepared for the day when Jay, Bob's best friend, phoned simply to ask her how she was holding up. As she drank in Jay's comfort over the phone, a frigid thorn of resentment crept into her heart. *Now, why can't Bob do this?* she wondered.

Things escalated with frightening speed. What began as innocent, therapeutic phone calls became lengthy conversations in person. Fueled by her desperate desire for companionship, Cathy soon found herself embroiled in a full-blown affair.

Her double life split her down the middle. On the one side, she was disgusted with her actions, sick with the knowledge of her unfaithfulness. But the other side of her relished the attention and affection Jay offered. His presence helped fill the emptiness inside her. So she stuffed her shame into a ball and hid it deep within the recesses of her heart, paving over her pain with substance abuse and the brief escape her times with Jay provided.

Life continued in this manner for three years, until one day when Cathy turned on the television and came across a Christian program. Something about the speaker's expression and sweeping voice caught her attention, and before she knew it she was totally focused on the screen, enraptured by the message of love and forgiveness that could be attained through a relationship with Jesus Christ.

Although she and Bob were active members in their church and had established deep, personal connections with their pastor and his wife, Cathy had never heard the message of salvation explained so clearly before. For years, she had sung the hymns and prayed the prayers. She had listened to the teachings of her pastors and studied the spirituality of her peers. Yet never had she cried out to God and felt adequately answered; never had she experienced for herself the power of a personal relationship with Jesus that she had heard so reverently described.

But that day, plagued by her sorrow and shame that still throbbed in her like an old wound, the speaker's words were infused with new life. They reached out to her, drawing her in, until she found herself kneeling on the living room floor, crying out to Jesus to enter her heart and save her from the terrible pain she held inside. And He did. She felt Him flowing through her soul like liquid light, throwing wide the darkened doors of her heart and cleansing her with peace.

The following day, eager to experience more of the program that had helped transform her life, Cathy flipped once again through the TV channels. She had never tuned in to that station before — and she never received it again.

Empowered by God's forgiveness, Cathy ended her affair with Jay. She believed that God had closed that part of her life for good, and neither she nor anyone else would ever have to revisit it again.

She had continued thinking that way until just hours before, when Jay's panic-stricken voice had lanced across the phone line, shattering her security with his news. His wife had found out about them.

Found out. The words pounded over and over through her brain as she numbly hung up the phone. She called her pastors and listened with mounting terror to their advice. And so now she stood in the shadowed doorway, grappling for the strength to stand before Bob and betray her secret and her marriage along with it.

COMING CLEAN

Cathy clenched her fists to keep them from trembling. Offering up one final, silent prayer, she approached her husband.

"Bob, I need to tell you something."

Her confession felt shapeless, soundless, as if her devastating words were formed from nothing but the thin air she was struggling to take in. They echoed off the walls, filling the space between them with their terrible roar, until finally she fell silent before her dumbfounded spouse.

Carefully, Bob came forward, moving closer and closer until she was forced to meet his eyes. There, to her astonishment, she saw not anger but compassion, not resentment but deep, unfathomable love. When he spoke, his voice was barely above a whisper, but it contained all the warmth and emotion she had felt when she first accepted Christ.

"Is *that* what you've been carrying around with you all these years?"

He folded her into his arms.

Cathy thought that was the end of it. After so many years of estrangement and silent pain, her burden had been lifted, and she nourished the hope that once again she could give herself wholeheartedly to her marriage. She never suspected that Bob would have secrets of his own to confess.

Less than twenty-four hours after Cathy's emotional declaration, it was he who stood before his wife, struggling for words. Bit by painful bit, his story came out. With their relationship fraying, Bob had given in to temptation. He confessed to Cathy that the last several years had been peppered with one-time flings, many induced by alcohol and all outside of their community.

Furthermore (they later deduced), Jay's wife had found out about Jay and Cathy long before she had confronted Jay with her knowledge. The woman's pain and rage had meshed into a quiet desire to see Cathy suffer as she had, and so she had begun to pursue Bob. Lost in his grief and alienated in his marriage, Bob had eventually given in to her persistence, resulting in a one-night stand with Jay's wife mere days before Cathy confessed.

For nearly seven years, Bob had harbored the searing shame of these moments of weakness within him, never dreaming that Cathy was living a lie that paralleled his own. When he had finished his account, Cathy greeted his acknowledgment of his guilt with the same devotion, compassion, and forgiveness he had shown her. That night, they held each other as they hadn't in years—without reservations, without fear. Their hearts were as new and exposed to one another as if they had been married only hours before.

In the following days, the pervading atmosphere of love and warmth continued to grow. Although their admissions had been terrible, the peace that washed over them afterward began to heal their wounds, soothing their previous pain like ointment. After years of secrets, the shadows that had stalked the edges of their marriage had been chased away by truth, and the very air seemed cleaner with relief.

REBUILDING

Despite this, Bob and Cathy knew that there was still progress to be made. The encircling wall of trust that they had built together had crumbled beneath the weight of their mistakes, and it would take time and effort to build it back up. In order to accomplish that, the couple committed themselves to a new standard of accountability. They regularly informed each other of where they were going and when. As their communication increased, the broken pieces of their faith in one another began to reform, becoming stronger with every new day.

In a further attempt at restoration, Bob and Cathy began counseling with their pastor and his wife. The emotional and spiritual guidance they received from their pastors proved to be essential to their healing process. This couple held Bob and Cathy to an even more rigorous standard of accountability while simultaneously coaching them in the ways of God's forgiveness and compassion. During this time, Bob made his own personal commitment to Christ, discovering for himself the power of God's redemption as his relationship with Cathy intensified with love and understanding.

The next twenty-five years would see the benefits of their salvation and their dedication to one another. To spare themselves unnecessary hurt, Bob and Cathy resolved to put their past behind them, recalling their testimony only to benefit other struggling couples with their own infidelity or similar marital problems. With God's help, Bob and Cathy were able to turn their previous pain into an instrument of love as they ministered to those suffering from the same pain that they themselves had experienced.

As time progressed, Bob sensed the spiritual call to enter pastoral ministry full-time. With God's guidance, he went on to found a new church in Maryland. He was later appointed the executive director of Marriage Savers of Frederick County in Maryland, an organization designed to help prepare couples for marriage and aid troubled spouses in salvaging their relationships.

Having trekked through thirty years of marriage, there came a day when, absorbed in some mental errand, Cathy found herself pausing once again in her doorway. Surrounded by memories, her fingertips glided across the painted wood, as if searching out traces of her former heartache in the grain. It wasn't there.

Instead, her heart pulsed with steady warmth, filling her with a sudden rush of gratitude for the enduring love she had experienced, both from her husband and from her Savior. She and Bob had stumbled so often in their walk together, their path lined with the jagged silhouettes of the obstacles that they had encountered. Yet out of the ruins of their mistakes, Christ had carved new words. Forgiveness. Mercy. Redemption. Release.

A smile played across Cathy's lips in the semi-darkness, the taste of the words like honey on her tongue. With a final, contented sigh she strode forward into the adjoining room, into the light.

—As told to Chelsea Apple

⨯

Bob Donk currently serves as the executive director of Marriage Savers of Frederick County, Maryland. Marriage Savers is an interfaith program operating in 200 cities throughout the United States and Canada. It is a community and congregational effort to actively reduce divorce rates locally and nationwide.

Communities instituting the Marriage Saver Community Marriage Policy programs find divorce rates dropping 17.5 percent on average. Cohabitation rates drop by a third. Additional programs provide mentoring to engaged couples, married couples, and blended families, giving them the skills, training, and support they need to build healthy relationships or even bring couples "back from the brink."

Marriage Savers of Frederick County
Rev. Robert J. Donk, Executive Director
10105 Kelly Road
Walkersville, MD 21793
(301) 898-8917

www.marriagesaversfrederick.org
bob@marriagesaversfrederick.org

Marriage Savers Inc. (National Office)
Mike and Harriet McManus
9311 Harrington Dr.
Potomac, MD 20854
(301) 469-5873
www.marriagesavers.org

Carmen was on autopilot as she drove laps around the neighborhood, crying and replaying the scene with Chris in her mind. What happened?

"You're leaving me?"

The clock didn't tick. No one breathed. At that moment Carmen couldn't have said where the kids were or even the color of Chris's shirt. Everything ceased to exist under the force of his calmly spoken words as they shattered her world. All her energy was focused on holding the tears back.

Chris turned away to reach into the drawer where the checks were kept. "It's already done. Where are the checks? I need one for a deposit on the apartment."

Carmen closed her eyes, asking God for the strength *not* to beg him to stay. What a reversal that would be. How many times her ex-husband, Ken, would hit her and call her names, and then beg for her not to leave him. When she opened her eyes again, Chris still stood there, close enough to touch—if touching could reach him. She crossed her arms. "Is there another woman?"

Silence.

Finally he spoke. "No, Carmen, there's not." There was a hint of sarcasm in his voice. "I just can't do this anymore."

Her body was numb, rooted to that one spot in the bedroom. She remembered how he kissed her so gently, making her feel precious for the first time in her life. "Chris, I love you. We can work through this."

But he just shook his head.

She sighed, beginning to grasp the ramifications of what was happening. "Well, if you're going to leave, *you* are going to have to go out there and tell the children. I won't do it for you." Carmen kept her voice low out of habit; they never fought in front of the children. They went for walks or drives or kept their arguments behind closed doors. It was one of the few things they were united on.

She turned to face the window, blind to the sun-filled day shining brightly outside. She heard him cross the bedroom and shut the door behind him. Woodenly, she walked to the bathroom and turned on the shower. There she collapsed, sobs wracking her body under the warm water.

Finally, she turned off the shower and wrapped herself in the hug of a soft, clean towel. Fingers trembling, she dialed a friend from church. "Linda, this is Carmen. Chris is leaving me."

• • •

Chris stood in the living room, unable to walk right in and tell the kids. Instead he paused, gazing at a picture frame. The lively eyes of Carmen's daughter and son, Michelle and Steven, smiled back at him through the glass.

These are our *children,* he thought. He'd already been separated from one child due to divorce and hated to see it happen again, but what could he do? *This isn't the life I wanted. She's always blaming me, accusing me. I can't even talk to another woman without her jumping all over me. She's so insecure. All we do is fight.*

His eyes fell on another picture: a tiny snapshot of a young woman and a baby tucked in the larger frame of Michelle's senior photo. The thought of Michelle's unexpected pregnancy was a blow to him all over again. He still didn't want to deal with it.

Things had never been the same between them after that, and he had pushed her away—something Carmen had a hard time understanding. It had nearly torn the family apart.

Steven . . . he was only thirteen now, but it seemed like the older he got, the more rebellious he became. For the past year, there'd been a lot of trouble, and raging hormones and girls chasing him didn't help matters. This wasn't the young man he knew Steven could be. This was not the son he used to build models with and cheer for when he'd earned new merit badges in Boy Scouts. He didn't have much in common with this boy searching so desperately for his identity. And the closeness they'd felt in years past was lost as they spent less and less time together.

And there was Carmen. A part of him wanted to go back, hold her, and tell her he didn't mean what he'd said. But he did mean it. It was just too difficult, one crisis after another. *Love won't fix this. I just want someone to listen to me and care about what I want for a change.*

He grabbed his suitcase and removed his car keys from his pocket. He strode to the front door and gripped the knob.

The phone rang.

It rang a couple more times before Chris reluctantly reached for it. "Hello?"

It was Loren, the husband of Linda, one of Carmen's best friends.

"Hey, Loren, this really isn't a good time."

Chris listened impatiently while Loren doggedly insisted they meet for coffee immediately. He suddenly had this urgent need to meet with Chris.

"Can't we do this some other day, Loren? What do you mean, no? Okay, maybe real quick, but this just isn't a good time for me. Okay, okay. I'll be there in twenty minutes."

• • •

Carmen combed her fingers through wet hair and started the car, hoping a drive would help her clear her mind. She was on autopilot as she drove laps around the neighborhood, crying and replaying the scene with Chris in her mind. *What happened?*

She had never expected to fall in love with Chris. When they first met, they were both married and had their own problems. All that time working at the phone company together, he'd seemed arrogant and wasn't very social.

Then one night Carmen's first husband had exploded in anger—again, and for the last time. Afterward she'd watched him load up for a camping trip. A couple of days later when he returned home and chucked his sleeping bag on the couch, the air of emptiness struck him: after thirteen years of abuse and fear, she was gone for good.

A year and a half later, Carmen heard that Chris's wife had left him. Knowing what it was like to be alone, she had felt sympathy. She almost laughed as she remembered thinking that since she wasn't really attracted to him, they could just be friends. But as she got to know him, she found out that he wasn't arrogant but gentle. Her attraction to him slowly grew, and soon they started dating.

Even so, she'd balked a little when he asked her on a "date" with his parents. *What is he—some kind of mama's boy?* But it wasn't anything like she'd expected. She loved being there and found herself wanting to be a part of them. There for visitation, Chris's only son ran around the apartment, charming each of the grandparents and Carmen in turn as only two-year-olds can do. She remembered the long-ago smallness of her own two children as she plopped him onto her lap.

Nothing about her dysfunctional upbringing had prepared her for this wholesome little sit-down. As they played cards, Carmen remembered her own childhood as one of many kids in an alcoholic, abusive family. Yet she'd felt so alone, so small amidst their lack of interest. In a way, she'd never really gotten to be a child; she had fended for herself from a young age and forged signatures on report cards that parents never asked for.

Then, as they sat there talking and laughing together, his parents asked her to bring her kids over so they could teach them to swim. She remembered how the tears filled her eyes as she finally felt a warmth that could include her *and* her children in a way that no one else had—not their father, not their own grandparents. These people she barely knew wanted her and the people she loved most to be a part of them.

She and Chris had gotten serious pretty quickly, and not everything about the relationship was perfect, but they were in love. In spite of the problems they were facing even then, they were certain this growing love would sustain them through anything that came their way. Chris started attending church with Carmen and her children despite his agnosticism. Five months into the relationship, they felt the pull of the Holy Spirit to come into a renewed relationship with God. A month after that, they were married. *We thought we'd live happily ever after . . .*

•   •   •

As Chris drove to the coffee shop, he couldn't help but think about the early days with Carmen. She was pretty and full of life, but she'd been hurt in so many ways by the people she was closest to. It had been hard for her to open up and trust, but he'd wanted to protect her—to make her feel special and beautiful. He couldn't believe the way he'd felt the first time she smiled at him . . . or the first time they kissed. He had felt a tidal wave of emotion.

The simplest things had made her happy. *Not anymore. These days, nothing I do seems right. She's always nagging me. And she lets the kids get away with too much.*

They had made a real effort to join together as a unit—thus the policy of arguing in private. They had also arranged visitation to give themselves maximum time as a family and as a couple, with Chris's son visiting on the weekends when Carmen's were home—and all of the kids gone on alternate weekends. The children were always "our children," but it was nice to have some time simply to be alone, to enjoy and get used to each other without all the responsibilities that come with a ready-made family.

And then there were the exes. *Why can't Carmen just tell him to leave us alone? There's no reason their conversations have to go on forever. I can't stand the way he talks to her and treats the kids. And she complains about me and* my *ex!*

Their methods of running a household were different too. Chris remembered with dismay the day he'd opened the pantry and discovered all the jars of store-bought spaghetti sauce. Disgusted, he threw them in the trash: clash one in the War of Different Expectations. *I wish she'd do things my way. I'm used to making homemade sauce—what's wrong with that? What's wrong with wanting things to be done right?* But when Carmen saw what he'd done, she confronted him. Hurt and angry, she felt criticized by his actions—rebuked for the way she, a working mother, managed the home.

The car in front of Chris was going way too slow. Irritation pulled him back to the present moment, and he pulled into a parking space beside the coffee shop. Once inside, he saw Loren sitting at a table not far away, focusing intently on his coffee. Sensing him, Loren looked up and waved, nudging the chair across from him with his foot.

"You can't just *leave* her, Chris," Loren said. "You have to step up and take responsibility for becoming the husband and father God intended you to be."

Chris was amazed by the straightforward audacity of this man—only an acquaintance—confronting him. But something of the conviction and authority in Loren's voice reached past Chris's wall. He began to really listen as Loren unrelentingly held him accountable for his promise to Carmen and his responsibility to his family, spiritually and practically, through all the landmines life put in their path. Laying it all on Carmen's shoulders so he could move on was not an option. Hearing the Spirit-led words, he knew Loren was right. He just didn't know what to do to face it.

●　●　●

That evening, Carmen moved about in a daze. The children came in and out of the rooms. They could see that something was wrong, but the expression on Carmen's face told them not to press for answers.

Sinking into the couch, Carmen watched her son sitting at the other end. How could she tell him the stepfather he'd grown up with wouldn't be around any more? She remembered the day they had told him about the engagement. While his sister danced around, all smiles, he had looked up at his mother with a face full of anguish and fear, asking, "Now that you're getting married, does that mean I'll never see my daddy?"

They had done their best to reassure him. Every other weekend, he went to visit his father. But every day in between, Chris worked to raise him and build a relationship with him. Chris got involved in his life, giving his time and enthusiasm to build something positive. Eventually, Steven learned to love and accept Chris, but it was so hard for him. *Was all his pain for nothing? Why can't Chris understand what he's putting us through? He just decides to leave and doesn't even give us a chance. I don't know why I should expect anything more; he always pulls away when things get hard.*

•   •   •

When Chris entered the bedroom that night, Carmen was already there, huddled tight with her back to him. The slightest quiver of surprise ran through her—wasn't he leaving?—but she didn't speak. What was left to say?

"I'm not leaving you," Chris whispered as he lay down beside her. "We have a lot of work to do, but I want to try." He leaned toward her, caressing her soft, dark hair and taking in the scent of her perfume, faint and warm.

And she turned to him, throwing herself into his arms once again. She didn't try to check the tears pouring down her face—tension released, transforming into liquid joy; he tasted the saltiness of her tears as he kissed her over and over, rejoicing with her and holding her tight.

•   •   •

Carmen finished telling her story, warmed by compassion as she looked across the table at the young couple they were counseling. Jeff and Susan stared back, hurt and animosity distorting their faces. "That night began the long journey of growing into the couple God meant us to be. It wasn't easy for us, and it won't be for you either. It took some serious marriage counseling and several years of seminars and small group study after that before we really began to work through our issues and learn to find our identity in Christ instead of each other—learning not to look to the other to complete us or to make us happy. No person can do that."

Chris joined her by saying, "We had to learn to see the strength our differences give us in communication, thinking, feeling, and handling problems . . . and in helping us understand the struggles other couples are going through." He squeezed Carmen's hand, loving the helper God had given him for this marriage ministry.

Twenty-six years of marriage . . . I never would have believed we'd get here. Carmen ran her thumb over the firm ridges of his fingers, loving the feel of the wedding ring pressing against her skin. "Life together isn't perfect. I'm still learning to let go of fears and insecurities that come from my past."

"But one of Carmen's biggest strengths is in confronting the tough issues and not letting them go until we solve them. Our family is better because she looks honestly at our problems. Don't pull away when Susan holds you accountable." Chris looked almost sheepish as he admitted, "I can be impatient with others' weaknesses; I see a little of that in you too, Jeff. But the flip side of that same quality can be perseverance to work through the obstacles and go the distance."

"We really do balance—and challenge—each other," Carmen mused. "There is satisfaction in supporting your husband, in meeting his needs and lending him strength. I never got that from waiting for him to make me happy and feel what I feel."

Chris looked thoughtful. "Her strengths . . . and weaknesses . . . complement mine and enable us to live and minister more fully. Without her there is no ministry." *Without her half of my heart is gone.* The smile in her eyes told him she had heard what he didn't say.

—As told to Lisa Holloway

◖•◗

Chris and Carmen Garner founded Fortified Marriages in an effort to assist married couples and churches seeking to build stronger marriages and families.

Chris and Carmen believe that a key element in constructing a good foundation for marriage is for each spouse to define his or her own identity and purpose in life, and then use that to build a mission in life together with his or her partner. Each spouse's differences can complement the other and give balance to the marriage relationship. Fortified Marriages also offers instruction for those wishing to start a couples' class or small group of their own.

Fortified Marriages
Chris and Carmen Garner
P. O. Box 7385
Chandler, AZ 85246
(480) 699-2515 or toll free (866) 263-5638
www.fortifiedmarriages.com
info@fortifiedmarriages.com

The counselor told them that Larry suffered from something called sexual addiction. *They had never heard of such a thing. They left that session laughing. How could one become addicted to sex?*

Larry's father was a traveling salesman, often gone on business from their West New York home. His mother was a homemaker who kept the family system neatly in order by making sure her rules were followed. Growing up with two emotionally distant parents, Larry felt isolated and disconnected from his family throughout most of his life.

By adolescence, he found himself searching for identity while also dealing with surging hormones and the social pressures of high school. He often felt alone and misunderstood. But rather than turning to his family for help, he sought it from like-minded friends at school. These friends provided Larry with a sense of community. They also provided him with other means of escaping his problems — he began experimenting with alcohol and drugs.

With addictive tendencies learned from his dysfunctional family system, Larry's time in high school continued in a downward spiral. What began as smoking in the bathroom and after-school drinking quickly escalated into LSD and cocaine use. Recreation soon became dependence. But the more drugs Larry used to escape his feelings of solitude, the more isolated he felt.

Toward the end of his junior year, Larry realized that drugs were taking over his life. His grades were plummeting, and his personal relationships were deteriorating. Even in the haze of his addiction he knew he had a decision to make: he could either continue down the path paved by the drugs, or he could turn things around and find a way to finally "get it right."

Before long, an opportunity presented itself: Army recruiters came to his high school. With a parent-signed waiver in hand, he enlisted on the spot. This was his chance to get away from his unhealthy circle of friends and start over. Instead of graduating with his classmates, Larry headed overseas for active duty in Germany. He hoped that the military service would bring about some much-needed change.

But on his very first night abroad, something unexpected happened that set him on the course for the rest of his life.

•   •   •

The barracks in Germany were barren and remote. Larry could get none of the usual contraband he had grown accustomed to. That first night he lay pensive in his bunk, his head buzzing, craving a fix to numb the loneliness that had haunted him for so long. As he stared at the blank ceiling, wondering what to do with himself now that the duties of his first day were completed, he found his options were limited.

Larry felt that familiar void as he lay motionless atop the stiff sheets. Sitting up, he scanned the room, and his eyes came to rest on something he recognized. There, lying on the floor in front of another recruit's trunk, were several pornographic magazines. Larry grabbed them and began flipping pages.

The images lent themselves to his senses, scratching the persistent itch left by his substance abuse. The women in those magazines seemed friendly and inviting, so unlike the stark, sanitized military environment that had engulfed him. During his next three years of service Larry came to depend on pornography as a "drug" that would always be available in the barracks.

Near the end of his first year in Germany, Larry was granted leave to visit his family. Upon arriving in the States, he felt just as alone as the day he had left. His new dependence upon pornography had grown strong, yet after reconnecting with his high school friends, his dormant addictions to cocaine and barbiturates resurfaced. After briefly reveling in his old habits, Larry returned to Germany with the same emptiness he had carried on his first trip.

Upon his arrival in Germany, Larry found himself depressed and reluctant to return to military life. So he wandered the famed red-light district of Frankfurt in search of something to fill the void in his restless and tormented soul.

The endless windows were lit by a warm, crimson glow, beckoning him from the cold, dirty streets of downtown Frankfurt. In his search for comfort and acceptance, he found a new "drug" in the form of a prostitute. She offered him a new "high," with an adrenaline rush that surpassed even the feelings provided by pornographic magazines and videos.

His feelings of emptiness now found a new outlet in the prostitute. Neither his guilt nor his fear could keep him from doing this. Afterward, Larry found himself guilt-ridden and ashamed, yet somehow energized. He desired more and began seeking it out whenever he could. For the next two years Larry was only working to play and playing to escape—always looking for another fix.

•   •   •

Four months before leaving the service, Larry and his unit opened their barracks for a Christmas party to support a local orphanage. With colorful ribbons and white plastic banners hung to welcome the children, the barracks held a refreshing air of excitement.

Larry was enjoying himself, sipping his German stout while roasting bratwursts on the grill. At one point during the party, a friend walked over to introduce his wife to Larry. Larry was pleased to meet her, but his interest quickly shifted to the couple's pretty friend standing close by. His friend introduced him to their friend Tania.

Larry was caught off-guard by Tania's red hair and stark blue eyes, which casually looked him over. He learned she was a nineteen-year-old American girl who had been living nearby with her German mother for the past eight years. After engaging her in some playful flirting, Larry refocused his interests in what carousing he could find for later that night.

As the party drew to a close, Larry and his friends headed out for some drinks at the local music bar. As usual, it wasn't long before Larry was drunk. Stumbling around the bar, he noticed Tania walk by. After a failed attempt to get her attention, he grabbed her by the hair and pulled her toward him as he slurred suggestive ramblings into her ear. Insulted and disgusted, Tania left the bar in a huff.

A few weeks after the orphanage function, Larry found that he needed some patches sewn onto his uniform. He knew that Tania had done similar work for a friend, so Larry asked his friend if he thought Tania might do the same for him. The friend informed Larry that Tania wouldn't work on his uniform until he apologized for his rude behavior at the bar.

Larry walked directly to her house to apologize in person. Tania was standing on the balcony of her mother's third story apartment. Larry called up to her from the street below. He hollered a quick expression of regret for disrespecting her at the bar, then invited her to dinner and maybe a walk in the park. Though hesitant, she agreed. She also agreed to do the sewing for him.

After that first date, the two began meeting on a regular basis. For the first time in years, Larry sensed he had found what he was searching for. Was it simply companionship? Or was it a true love, an intimacy and transparency that might finally fill the void in his soul?

As Larry's enlistment in Germany drew to a close, the couple had to make a decision as to where their relationship was headed. They decided to stay together, and Tania agreed to move back to the United States with Larry. Just a few months after their first date, they were living together in coastal southwest Florida, engaged to be married. The young couple was in love and optimistic about the future. But it wasn't long before Larry's addictions surfaced yet again.

•   •   •

Tania had seen her share of pornography in the sexually uninhibited culture of central Europe. So for a while she didn't think twice about seeing Larry's magazines and videos around the house. But she had no idea how serious Larry's issues were.

Soon pictures and videos were not enough to satisfy Larry, and he resorted to phone sex calls. The peculiar phone numbers and credit card charges told an all too familiar tale. Distraught, Tania confronted Larry and insisted they see a professional counselor.

After listening to Larry and Tania talk about their persisting issues, the counselor told them that Larry suffered from something called *sexual addiction*. They had never heard of such a thing. They left that session laughing. How could one become addicted to sex? As a result of the visit, Larry gave up drug abuse for good.

But pornography would prove much harder to let go of.

Before long, Larry was caught up in his secret world once again. Lies to keep his behavior hidden became commonplace. Tania suspected. She sensed a growing distance between them. Further, though she knew about the phone calls, she was curious about why he'd been spending so much time at the computer lately. She began to investigate his online activities.

She discovered that Larry had begun using Internet chat rooms as a new way to connect with women. Tania was beside herself when faced with the black-and-white proof of Larry's infidelity.

She confronted Larry about his addictions yet again. This time she sought help for them from a professional psychologist. While this provided some temporary relief, Tania grew suspicious again just two years later; she asked Larry if he had relapsed. He answered honestly. He had once again been feeding his addiction in secret.

Tania was devastated. She had trusted that Larry had overcome this problem on his own. Not knowing where else to turn, Tania decided to seek answers from their local church. Both Larry and Tania had been raised Catholic, but neither had been to church since they were children. Their new church provided them with recovery assistance, but a piece of the puzzle was still missing.

Larry and Tania had both recommitted themselves to church and had become active in ministry. They even made prayer and devotional time an everyday practice. Yet Tania still struggled with intense feelings of betrayal. Neither of them had truly come to understand faith's central role in healing. They hadn't yet grasped how selfless they were being called to be. As a result, Larry soon fell back into his old ways.

They weren't sure what the answer was, but they both knew that something had to drastically change, or their relationship would soon be over. They thought again of what that first counselor had said. This sent them rushing to the local library for answers. There they found as much literature on sexual addiction as they could get their hands on. But after a desperate search for local resources and small groups, they found the area had little to offer.

Soon Larry got a job that required long hours in front of a private computer. It was like putting an alcoholic behind a bar. Sure enough, Larry found himself unable to control his actions. Finally Larry realized that this *thing* was much more than a habit—or even an addiction. It was a disease. And by now he understood that he couldn't shake it off by himself.

• • •

Larry and Tania changed churches and decided to give faith another chance. They were ready to confess their struggles to God and earnestly ask for help. They approached their pastor and told him everything. They were willing to do whatever it took to find healing.

Even though they were expecting to hear the same advice they had found on Internet sites and in professional therapy, they nevertheless clung to a quiet hope for some relief. To their surprise, the pastor directed them to another couple with a story similar to theirs. The couple shared information about an organization called Bethesda Workshops, which offers intensive workshops for those struggling with sexual addictions.

Finally they were no longer alone. Others were suffering just as they were. This gave them hope that their future was *not* determined. Perhaps pornography's grip on their relationship could be broken after all.

The workshops were held in Nashville, almost nine hundred miles from their home in Florida. It didn't matter; they were going. They decided to send Larry first, to attend the men's workshop.

Tania would attend a spouse's workshop a week later. Then the following week they would board a plane together and return to Bethesda for a couples' workshop.

In total, the conferences lasted three weeks. With all the time they would have to take off from work, they found the total cost of travel, lodging, and admission far exceeded their budget. Even so, they decided that their healing would be worth the sacrifice.

Larry and Tania thought about refinancing their home to pay for the trip, but then decided to apply for a home equity loan. They applied in good faith, but were unsure of the outcome. Soon they received a reply from the bank. To their surprise, the closing banker drove two hours through a stormy night to sign the loan approval on their kitchen table. They took the approval as a sign that they were headed in the right direction.

With the loan, they finally had enough money for the workshops. Larry flew to Nashville. It was there that he felt God really moving in his life for the first time. With a profusion of counselors and speakers, plus twelve hours of therapy a day, Larry was hard at work. At one point he took a deep breath and looked toward a picture of Jesus on the wall. *Recovery is a process,* he reminded himself, *not an event.* Clearly, it would be a long road to recovery, and only with hope and faith would it be possible.

During one of the presentations, Larry was asked to close his eyes and think about his life's mission. Not expecting much, he compliantly shut his eyes. He then came to a surprising realization. Perhaps it could be his mission to take this message of hope and healing to others.

At the end of the first week, Larry took his new understanding of personal hope and salvation back to Tania in Florida. She was overjoyed with the dynamic results she saw in her husband. Then it was her turn. She flew to Nashville for the spouse's workshop.

Being a "co-addict" for so long had been hard on Tania. She

was hurting just as much as Larry, but in different ways. This ongoing struggle was the hardest thing she had ever dealt with. Until this point, her search for support had been disheartening, and her journey had become a lonesome one. But after arriving in Nashville, she soon felt the warmth of the conference's community blanketing that chill of isolation. She found that there were people who cared about her and understood her struggles.

The week was as enlightening as her husband's had been. Before she left, she bought as many books as would fit in her luggage; she returned to Florida with a mantra of her own: "Let go and let God."

The next week, as planned, they left for Nashville together. In the couples' workshop Larry and Tania became a team. "Allies, not enemies" became their motto. They learned to love one another for who they were, erasing the fantasy of what they had wished the other to be. They finally came to understand the meaning of unconditional love, which meant loving each other "warts and all." In the weeks and years to come, they became more transparent with each other, knowing that nothing could be allowed to remain hidden between them, no matter how embarrassed or ashamed they felt.

While at the workshops, Tania and Larry found CDs, tapes, and workbooks from an organization called "LIFE Ministries." LIFE Ministries, they learned, was a Christ-centered support group and recovery ministry based in Orlando, Florida. Finally, they had found solid resources close to home. They decided that the work they had done during those past weeks was only the beginning. The workbooks would offer a way to continue living in freedom every day.

The overwhelming message of the workshops was that the power of Christ is essential to breaking the corrupted chains of sexual dependence. They knew they needed a power greater than themselves to fight this battle.

Looking back on his life, Larry began to realize that even though he had never gone to prison, he had become imprisoned to himself. Since his youth he had been pushing away the very freedom he desired. In the end, it was the love of a woman and the love of his Father that finally brought him to it.

—As told to Patrick Womack

⟲•⟳

Larry Gaudieri currently serves as the Director of Leadership Development for LIFE Ministries. This sexual addiction recovery ministry seeks to break isolation and bring freedom to those suffering from sexual brokenness.

LIFE offers workbook resources, leadership training, support group structures, and much more. Their nationwide support groups employ Dr. Mark Laaser's seven principles of sexual addiction recovery to help men and women learn how to live their lives in freedom every day.

LIFE (Living in Freedom Everyday) Ministries
(866) 408-LIFE
www.freedomeveryday.org

How dare he do this to me and our children? If he really cared about his family, couldn't he make himself get better faster? Why wouldn't he stop threatening the total disruption of my tidy life?

Tears streamed down Kevin's face. "I can't do it anymore, Angie."

It would have been one thing if he had told me this in our home, in private. But he was standing in the pulpit saying this to me—in front of his entire congregation, in the middle of his Sunday morning sermon.

Kevin stumbled down from the platform and collapsed on the front bench. I met him there as family, friends, and other leaders surrounded us. My mind was whirling, but I knew I had to get him out of that crowd. I switched into emergency mode, put all other thoughts aside, and helped Kevin to the car. I don't remember if I gathered my things, but somehow I found the car keys. The rest is blank, except for the overwhelming feelings of disaster and dread.

Why was this happening to us? How were we going to get over this, whatever *this* was? When could we face the congregation that had just watched my husband collapse emotionally and spiritually? These questions would soon fade in light of something much more serious.

How Did We End Up Here?

We spent the remainder of the day trying to figure out how we had arrived in this dark state. As we discussed our lives, we realized that Kevin was suffering from severe burnout and high stress. He lacked the strength and will to continue on with life. I knew he had been dealing with stress and needed a change, but we hadn't truly altered anything until now. This crisis was forcing us to take a look at the mess our lives had become. We cried, confused and directionless. Concern for our two children in grade school and middle school hovered at the edge of our conversations.

Our church family was a real help to us then. Church leaders immediately granted Kevin time off to seek counseling and recover. As the hours stretched into days and then months, our church continued to give us full paychecks so we would not have added financial stress. Family, friends, and church members gathered around us—physically, emotionally, and spiritually—and prayed for us. Many wanted to help, but they respected our need to be alone.

Much later, we found out that God had made connections in advance to provide help. Unbeknownst to us, there was a visitor at church that Sunday morning. She regularly attended another church in our valley, but she was convinced by God that she must go to our church that specific day. After witnessing Kevin's collapse, she called her pastor. This godly appointment was the first step on the road of recovery for the Quantrell family, although we didn't know it at the time.

As God had planned it, the fellow pastor knew of a helper, Dr. Gary Pinion ("Dr. P," as we call him now). He has a specific calling to reach out to pastors and leaders in crisis. His ministry fit our situation perfectly. My husband, Pastor Kevin, was definitely in crisis. Someone contacted Dr. P, and he called us right away.

When we spoke with Dr. Pinion, he immediately recognized our circumstances and referred us to a Christian counselor he knew in Seattle.

Ed Davis was yet another provision in God's plan for help. Prior to our meeting, Ed and his wife, Diane, had felt called by God to help married couples in trouble. Heeding the call, they had recently remodeled an apartment over their garage. This provided a retreat space for couples as they received counseling from Ed and Diane. We were their first attempt at residential marriage intervention — the guinea pigs!

By this time, Kevin was in terrible condition. He hated getting out of bed and wanted the curtains closed and the lights off. I was the only person he wanted to talk to. He slept all the time. He quit eating. His clothes began to hang off of him, and I had to practically force nourishment into his mouth. He was consumed with misery. But even so, I don't think he realized how ill he was. He knew only that life had lost its appeal. He was clearly trapped in a dark depression. So, with nerves jangling, we traveled to Ed and Diane's house for a weekend of intense counseling.

GETTING SOME PERSPECTIVE

That Saturday morning we followed Ed to his office for what would prove to be a day of painful and emotional counsel.

One of the first things Ed advised us to do was see our family doctor and begin medical treatment for depression. He actually encouraged both of us to seek medicinal support. Although Kevin was the one with major depression, I would soon have to deal with my resulting depression, stress, and anxiety as I cared for him and the rest of the family. When we returned home, we were both prescribed antidepressants.

As we spoke with Ed, Kevin and I began to see how far apart

we had drifted from each other. Kevin worked full-time as a pastor, a job fraught with long hours, round-the-clock phone calls, and crisis situations; he was constantly dealing with church management, difficult people, sick people, and spiritual attacks from all sides. He was also a volunteer firefighter, which kept him away from home even more. As the spiritual leader of our church family, Kevin constantly faced the sins and disasters present in the lives of others. Add to that his own family and home responsibilities, and his plate was overflowing.

I was the proverbial working mom. With a husband who was often gone or distracted, it was my responsibility to care for our two children, tend to our extended family, and manage the home. Combined with my church responsibilities, writing, and teaching full-time, my hands were just as full as my husband's. Every second of my day was overscheduled. Each night, late, Kevin and I would collapse into bed, exhausted.

This did not contribute to a loving, supportive, healthy marriage. "Us time" was nonexistent. In hindsight, we should have been wiser, but we were not. We were trying to be the perfect pastor's family, but for us it spelled disaster.

During counseling with Ed and Diane we learned about depression and burnout and the effects of each. Around this time, Kevin was also diagnosed with obsessive-compulsive disorder, which causes a person to be perpetually stuck in a rut, thought, or habit. This made his depression worse, since he would get caught in a cycle of despair or continually focus on a negative event. The OCD made it impossible for him to break out of the thought pattern and think of anything else. We filled out questionnaires, completed homework, and prayed together.

Dr. P, Ed, and Diane became my unbiased sounding boards, and I often conferred with them for suggestions or confirmation of choices. Kevin and I spent hours, sometimes two or three times a day, walking along the mile-long ditch near our home. The sounds of nature, running water, and sunshine nurtured our injured souls. The healing stretched from weeks into months, but all the while, our families, friends, and church stood beside us and continued to pray and offer help.

During this slow, agonizing process, I often found myself overwhelmed. I was now caring for my home, my children, *and* Kevin. I had taken over many of his prior responsibilities. I drove him to and from counseling sessions. I spent hours talking things through with him. But I was growing sick of the same conversations, the same reasons, the same sentences. Kevin's OCD forced us to revisit each thought numerous times.

I resented him for his failure to do what I expected from a partner. And though I tried not to show it, I was angry at Kevin for breaking down and upsetting our family. With the depression, we no longer had a sex life, so physical intimacy was absent. Our lives were less than pleasant. Nevertheless, I felt strengthened by God and the support and prayers of others, and I held on.

A Set-up for A Breakdown

Looking back, we should have seen that a breakdown was due to happen for one of us. Kevin, my best friend and husband of seventeen years, grew up as an only child, and a cherished one. Add a type-A personality and overactive work ethic, and Kevin was almost guaranteed to have some issues. I was the oldest child, an overachieving perfectionist. This eldest daughter wanted to please everyone, including parents, teachers, peers, and employers.

Neither Kevin nor I had the ability to say no. We overextended our boundaries to please as many people as possible and habitually said yes before thinking through our real-life schedule and the consequences of overbooked days, evenings, and weekends.

We struggled. As we spoke with Ed, Diane, and Dr. P, we discovered that we had to put a stop to our endless busyness and time away from each other. We were married, but in reality we were merely coexisting, running parallel to each other rather than side by side, holding hands. In those precious weekend sessions, we learned so much about ourselves, our marriage, and our personalities. We were finally learning how to build a healthy relationship.

A CLOSE CALL

But God was not yet done with our lessons. I was still holding on to the "I can do it myself" attitude. But one morning, after my day as a preschool teacher had just begun, I got a phone call from Kevin. He'd still been in bed when I left for school. Our children were also at school, so he was home alone. Normally, I did not take personal calls when preschoolers were present. But something in my co-worker's face filled me with foreboding, so I took the call.

With anxiety borne in the root of my being, I held the receiver to my ear.

"Angie, I need help," came the weak and tormented voice. "I'm holding the gun, and I can't trust myself to not end it all."

Suddenly, my preschool problems seemed irrelevant. My world came tumbling down. Again. "Don't do anything," I said. "I'm on my way."

My co-worker saw the blood drain from my face. I was frozen in terror. Fifteen preschoolers looked at me, but I barely noticed. "Go," she said.

"Call the office," I said. Then I leaned in to whisper to her. "He has a gun."

That short ride home, less than two miles, took an eternity. Would I find bits and pieces of blood and brains all over my bedroom? Would Kevin be holding the gun to his head, poised to pull the trigger when I walked in? Would I hear the sound of a gunshot ring through our quiet neighborhood?

But then my terror was overshadowed by rage. How dare he do this to me and our children? If he really cared about his family, couldn't he make himself get better faster? Why wouldn't he stop threatening the total disruption of my tidy life?

"Kevin?" I screamed as I entered our house. "What are you doing?"

No answer came. I braced myself for what I would see and began the walk to our bedroom, the furthest room from the front door. I had my cell phone in my hand and 911 all but dialed.

I opened the door to our bedroom and found Kevin lying in bed, the gun beside him on the comforter. He was alive. As my fear dissipated, my anger took over. I grabbed the gun and started yelling at him, fear and rage pouring out. I think I may have made up some colorful words that day.

I started dictating. "Get out of bed and get dressed. I can't deal with this anymore. You are going to the hospital."

I dragged him to the car and began driving to the mental hospital in a large town near us.

"What do you think you are doing?" I asked. "Do you want our children to find you like this? How do you think this makes me feel? I can't believe you are doing this!"

It was easy for me to blame him for everything. But mental illness causes individuals to do things they would not normally do.

Kevin checked himself into the mental ward of the hospital and spent the weekend as a patient on suicide watch.

I cried all the way home and then set about removing weapons and sharp objects from the house and giving them to my sister. I shared my struggles with her. I talked to a few trusted others too. I found outlets to spill my pain, as Kevin wasn't in a position to listen to what I was going through. At the hospital Kevin received counsel and group therapy, while I received encouragement and help from Dr. P and Ed.

This was our absolute lowest point. We were forced to rely on God and the people He had provided for our assistance.

WE'RE NOT SUPERHEROES

Our pride was smashed. We had mistakenly believed that we could do the life of the "super-pastor family" alone, without God's (or anyone else's) help. Our God-given leadership skills were overworked and pushed with our own desires and choices. We had foolishly filled our days and calendars with what we thought we needed to do, not necessarily what God wanted us to do. God woke us up so we could stop blindly doing things for Him and finally start *listening* to Him.

We never thought this could happen to us. But it did. It can happen to anyone.

Slowly we began to heal. The wisdom we've gained is priceless, but the journey to it was excruciating. As Kevin and I began working again toward recovery, we spent hours working to forgive each other for the things, little and great, that we had done, unknowingly and knowingly, to hurt each other throughout our marriage. Because we were still best friends, we were able to salvage the good and throw out the rest, knowing that one day the lessons we had learned would be used to help others.

Of the many things Kevin and I learned during this trial, the most important was depending on God and praising Him. Our relationship with God and each other grew tremendously. We also learned that close friends and confidants are vital. Help is also available from professionals, and God often puts Christian assistance in our path precisely when we need it.

Kevin and I discovered that we have to continually work on

our marriage and prioritize our family. We learned the importance of making good choices and setting boundaries for the expectations of others on our lives. Exercise, a healthy diet, and "us time" are all necessities. Prayer is a vital and daily need, and patience is required for ourselves and for each other.

We can easily say this time was the most difficult, scary, stressful, and horrible of our married lives. Yet in the same breath, we say it has become the best event of our marriage. We see it now as an opportunity for renewed commitment and growth as individuals and as a couple. We know that God used this time to get our hearts out of the world and into Him.

We learned to hang on, because hope is a reality. The One who brought us through all of it is able to help in any situation. The Bible became my foundation, prayer and journaling my source of processing my pain and letting the power of the Lord heal me and guide me. In those dark days, I kept telling myself, "Five years from now, things will be much better."

Now more than five years later and twenty-two years into our marriage, our relationship is healthier and stronger than ever. Kevin and I still struggle with overbooking our lives, but God has given us wisdom for pruning commitments and focusing on family and Him. It is with much amazement and joy we see how God prepared to care for us, even before we knew we needed care and help. He taught us about Himself, others, life, depression, choices, sin, forgiveness, and love. What an awesome God!

—Angie Quantrell

∞ • ∞

Angie and Kevin Quantrell found much-needed help in their time of crisis through the outreach of Encouragement Dynamics. Encouragement Dynamics is a ministry that focuses on helping hurting pastors and their families as they deal with today's ministerial environment, which can often be overwhelming.

Founded and directed by Dr. Gary Pinion, author of the book, *Crushed,* this "ministry of encouragement" is a three-part effort providing restoration, motivation, and education as it aids pastors and their families in their recovery from troubles in life and ministry.

Encouragement Dynamics
2919 Troon Court
Richland, WA 99354
(509) 521-5014
www.encouragementdynamics.com
gpinion@aol.com

BOB *and* AUDREY

Had I understood and practiced the principle of covering my
wife and family, the adultery might never have occurred.

A dultery.
     We never dreamed it could happen to us. We had it all: a "perfect" marriage, three beautiful kids, a fruitful television ministry, and above all else, a deep love for Jesus. Our course was set and our way seemed sure. The forecast: calm seas ahead. Infidelity was not even a cloud on the horizon. Or so we thought.

It all began so gradually. Seeming innocent at first, sin slowly drew me (Audrey) off the true path and onto a trail of lies and self-deception. Against my conscience and better judgment, I made one small compromise after another, smugly confident that I could handle it.

Self-deception really messes with the mind. During all this time, my love for Bob and my commitment to our marriage never wavered. At the same time, I wanted to keep my new secret relationship that seemed so exciting. In my foolishness and selfishness, I thought I could have both.

I never knew true pain until the day I confessed my adultery to the person I loved the most. The tidal wave of disbelief, horror, and anger threatened to completely envelop me and choke the life out of me. In that moment I began to understand the magnitude of my sin.

We were alone in a small office. It was quiet and still. I was sitting on the floor holding Bob's feet. My heart was beating so fast that my hands were shaking. Slowly, I let the dreaded words escape from my mouth. Bob responded with shock and disbelief. I just sat and wept quietly. I knew my confession would hurt Bob, but I had no idea of the depth of pain he would suffer. If I had realistically considered Bob's feelings in the beginning, I'm sure I wouldn't have done what I did in the first place. At any rate, I was totally unprepared for what happened next.

Bob stood up and walked out. He simply left the room. I cupped my face in my hands and felt extremely alone. *Would Bob come back? What if he didn't? If he did, what would he say? What would he do?*

BOB

What should I do? Where should I go? My first impulse was to run, to go somewhere—anywhere—to get away from Audrey and the horrible reality that I could not yet face.

My next impulse was to tell everybody I saw about what had happened, to broadcast my innocence and to point to Audrey as the evil one who had betrayed her husband. I wanted to shout, "See what she did to me!"

Of course I wasn't thinking clearly right after I walked out on Audrey. I was absolutely clueless about what to do and unable to make decisions on my own. All I knew was I needed help and I needed it fast. I went into my office, shut the door, and immediately pulled a book from my shelf: *Is God in Your Marriage?* by Pastor Leo Godzich.

Several years earlier, Leo and his wife, Molly, had been guests on our television program. We had all hit it off that morning but hadn't kept in touch. I wondered what suddenly drew me to Leo's book.

Almost in a daze I pulled Leo's phone number in Phoenix,

Arizona, from the back of his book, dialed it, and waited anxiously as the call rang through.

Voice mail.

I couldn't believe it. Here I was in crisis, and Leo was at lunch! All I could do was leave a message. Finally, my phone rang. It was Leo's office. I quickly filled him in on the situation. They immediately recognized that I needed someone to guide me through this minefield because I was in no condition to find my own way. When Leo got on the line, I frantically asked him what I should do.

"The first thing you do is get back into that bed with Audrey tonight. Don't spend one night apart from each other. Not one."

I couldn't believe it. "You've got to be kidding!"

"I'm not saying you have to have sex, but you will not defile that marriage bed. Do not sleep apart. You are not going to be a part of this divorce culture."

I listened, but I still felt like running.

"Bob, I know you feel like your flesh is ripped open. I know you feel devastated. But the question is, what are you going to do about it? Are you going to protect and *cover* your wife and children? Are you going to *cover* your marriage?"

Leo explained that concealing this matter was not to cover it *up*, but to cover it so that healing could take place. Leo informed me that despite my feelings of the moment, it was my responsibility to cover Audrey rather than expose her.

Leo may have hit me pretty hard, but he didn't let Audrey off the hook. He said the first thing she needed to do was tell her parents.

AUDREY

I told my parents the next day. Next to confessing to Bob, confessing to my parents that I had committed adultery was the hardest thing I have ever done.

As I poured out the truth to each of them, I saw the intense hurt in their eyes.

I asked them to forgive me, and they did. Mom and Dad each separately reassured me that their love was unconditional and that they would do anything humanly possible to get us through this crisis.

Soon after, Bob's pain and anger spilled over into a tsunami of emotion flung in my direction. Suddenly, it was all about questions. Bob already knew the "who" of the affair. Now he demanded to know when and where and how many times. He wanted to know if I enjoyed it and if I loved this other man.

With every new confession I tried to appease Bob's mind, but I knew my answers were not what he wanted to hear. He desperately wanted to believe that I was a helpless victim and not a willing participant. That way he would have an excuse to release me from responsibility and could focus all of his wrath on the other person. I wanted to lie to make everything all right. However, I could not give Bob the answers he was looking for. I was responsible, and I knew it.

When Bob first contacted him, Leo was involved in a pastor's conference in Phoenix. Despite his busy schedule, Leo knew that Bob and I shouldn't be alone. He insisted that we fly to Phoenix, where his church would put us up for the week and he would talk with us as he could.

The day after I confessed my adultery to Bob, on the evening of the same day I told my parents, Bob and I boarded a flight to Phoenix, Arizona.

What lay ahead? God alone knew.

We flew from Winnipeg to Toronto, where we had an all-night layover. Bob sat in the row across from me and stared at me. I couldn't even imagine what he was thinking or feeling.

BOB

The night Audrey and I spent in the Toronto airport was probably the longest night of my life. As I sat there, watching her, my mind was conflicted. I loved her. But the questions! The pain! The confusion! But mostly the anger. It swept over me like a wave, then receded, only to return and wash over me again with the same intensity as before.

When we arrived in Phoenix, Leo's assistant picked us up at the airport. Our destination was a beautiful resort in Phoenix, courtesy of Leo's Sunday school class. In spite of all the beauty and luxury surrounding us, the one thing on our minds was seeing Leo.

Despite his busy schedule that week, Leo spent as much time with us as he could. He counseled us in several areas, but more than anything he continued to stress the importance of *covering* in our relationship and in this situation.

Without a doubt, Audrey was accountable to God for her actions. But I had to acknowledge the unpleasant truth that my lack of spiritual diligence had also contributed to what happened. Had I understood and practiced the principle of covering my wife and family, the adultery might never have occurred.

It was my lack of understanding of the covering principle that also caused me at first to want to tell everybody what Audrey had done and to declare my own innocence. But God's desire for our situation was healing and restoration, which started with concealing or covering it for protection.

God designed every woman with a deep desire to be covered. Every man is designed by God to be a coverer, a protector and provider for his wife and children. Part of the man's function is to be a buffer between his family and the harshness of the world.

One day late in the week of our visit to Phoenix, a thought suddenly occurred to me, and I was hit with my first panic attack.

What if Audrey's pregnant?

Terrified, I shared my fear with Leo. He replied calmly, "When the time comes, God's grace will be sufficient."

I felt like punching him.

I couldn't see it then, but I can say today with complete assurance that God's grace *is* sufficient. At that time I had only begun seeing beyond myself. So much of what I'd always believed to be true was being tested. But today, Audrey and I have allowed grace to be perfected in our weakness and have come to know the love of our heavenly Father as never before.

AUDREY

A few weeks after returning to Winnipeg, I missed my monthly cycle. I tried to dismiss my fears, but after using two home pregnancy kits with unclear results, we took a trip to the walk-in clinic. Bob and I sat together in the doctor's office when he informed us of the news.

"The test came back positive. Do you want to continue the pregnancy?"

I felt Bob's pain at that moment, but for the first time in weeks I also felt his strength. Every bit of strength I could muster to face this new reality was not enough. I was completely spent. After I'd committed adultery and confessed—and now with a baby on the way—I didn't think I could face life.

In that instant, our lives changed. Gone was our goal of trying to keep ourselves together and get through the pain without hurting others. Questions jumped into our heads like popcorn: How do we quit the church? Whom do we tell? Where do we go? What do we do with the baby?

It would have been so easy to have an abortion and let things go on as if nothing had happened. One day I even made an anonymous phone call to find out what the procedure would be. The woman I spoke to said casually that since my pregnancy had been detected so early, I could simply take ten pills and the baby would be gone. I cried and repented to God for even making the phone call.

When Bob called Leo, frantic for advice, he was met with a direct challenge. "You have a decision to make, Bob. Fatherlessness is the plague of this generation. You can either contribute to the fatherlessness, or you can choose to be conformed to the character of your Creator, who is Father to the fatherless."

It was an easy answer. It was the right answer. But it wasn't an easy one to live out during a nine-month pregnancy. Doing the right thing is not always easy.

Bob and I decided that we needed to leave Winnipeg, at least for a while. We would move to a safe location where we would be covered and could begin rebuilding our lives while protecting our children. The safe choice was Phoenix, the scene of our initial rescue.

Our children embraced the move with the typical youthful excitement over something new. Of course, they knew nothing as yet of the adultery or the baby. Bob and I wanted to carefully and lovingly prepare just the right environment in which to tell them.

Life suddenly became a whirlwind for us. There was much to do. We had to sell our house, quit our church, and pack up our children and belongings and haul them off to a strange new city.

BOB

When we arrived in Phoenix, God graciously provided us with a home, a welcoming church family, and a means of income. Once we were settled, it was time to tell our children what was going on.

Our biggest concern was what exactly we should tell them. After discussing it at length, Audrey and I both felt they needed to know that another person was involved. We didn't want them to one day feel betrayed because we hadn't shared the truth with them.

As a husband, my challenge was to bring covering, healing, and wholeness to what sin had eroded and infected. My children are under my covering until the day they leave my home, marry and make a home of their own. Until that time, I am responsible to God for how I cover them.

AUDREY

Telling our children was a sobering event. We painstakingly went through each detail of how and when we would tell them. Bob and I knew it would be a defining moment in their lives. We knew that they would most likely adopt our perspective, so how we communicated the news was of utmost importance. If we told them this was a terrible thing, they would automatically shift into that paradigm. Yet the sin *was* terrible. But, as always, God is faithful. He used Bob in a powerful way to demonstrate His character.

The kids gathered upstairs in our bedroom and we all sat on the carpet. Bob had a huge blanket and wrapped it over me like a tent. He then held me close to his chest. "Kids," he said, "take a look at this picture. Whenever we make a mistake and we go to our heavenly Father to ask forgiveness, He embraces us, holds us close, and covers us with His love just like I'm covering your mom."

Bob then assured the children that we were a family and there was *nothing* that would break us apart or cause their Mom and Dad to separate. He then simply said that I had made a great mistake and that they were going to have a baby brother. I did not know ahead of time that he was going to cover me. I felt so loved and cared for! The kids didn't have to see my face as Bob explained what happened. We knew they would eventually have questions, but that night we were all comforted as we sensed God covering us as His family.

Afterwards, there was perfect peace in the room. Tears ran down our cheeks, and we all held each other. The children embraced one another with complete acceptance and excitement. Certainly, our kids had to deal with feelings that only they could talk about, but God answered our prayers in keeping them all strong and secure.

Our family was intact, and it was only by the grace of God. We were *covered*!

BOB

Audrey's water broke eight months into the pregnancy, and when the baby — *our* baby — boy was born, I gave him my name — Robert Theodore Meisner. I didn't want him to ever question whose boy he was. He is my son, and he is a divine gift. God knew exactly what I needed to deal with the issues in my heart. As I have allowed God to love me unconditionally and extravagantly, I, in turn, can effortlessly love this little boy, *my* son.

AUDREY

Our journey of healing has taken years and has come in layers. Just two years after Robert was born, we experienced a monumental weekend in God's presence. By divine appointment, another couple in ministry prayed over us. While they didn't know our story of crisis, after praying, they sensed that I was suffering from acute grief. I told them of the loss that had occurred, and it became obvious that I had still not forgiven myself for what I had done.

As we prayed together, a miracle took place. I began to see how God viewed me. I clearly heard Him ask me, "Audrey, will you receive what I paid dearly for? Will you be obedient in seeing yourself as I see you? Completely clean and perfectly beautiful." In that moment, my heart changed, and shame was removed. From that day forward I no longer accept the judgment of others. I am free!

BOB

We also spent some time dealing with *my* issues. I remember crying as I sorted through the images I had created in my mind while imagining Audrey with this other person. Every time before, when I visualized the actual moment when Audrey became pregnant, I saw myself standing over her, pointing my finger at her in judgment.

But this night was different. This time, I saw Jesus behind me, asking, "Bob, with love in your heart, will you reach down and take her to yourself and rescue her?" I said yes, and my heart changed. That night we fell into each other's arms feeling safe and secure, healed and loved. We have enjoyed a transparent and intimate relationship as best friends ever since.

BOB AND AUDREY

As we write this, Robert is turning six years old. He is happy, beautiful, funny, talented, and deeply loved. He smiles even in his sleep. He loves God with all his heart. Our family is healed and whole. All four children still live at home, the two oldest attending college nearby. We laugh and dream together every day. We know that it's by God's grace that we are united as a family.

—Bob and Audrey Meisner

Excerpts from "Marriage Under Cover" used with permission
of the authors and Milestones International Publishers.

☙ • ☙

Bob and Audrey Meisner are the authors of the books *Best Friends, Best Lovers* and *Marriage Under Cover.* They travel the country communicating their miraculous story of restoration after adultery and an unplanned pregnancy. They are also frequent guest speakers at NAME conferences.

Their mutual dream is to see all married couples experience relationships filled with friendship, peace, joy, shared dreams, and shared laughter.

www.bobandaudrey.com
Audrey@bobandaudrey.com
Bob@bobandaudrey.com

They thought that the lessons from their past marriages and divorces had taught them everything they needed to know to make this partnership last a lifetime.
They were wrong.

When Joe and Michelle met in the early 1980s, they had a total of seven divorces between them. Not only that, but Michelle also had three children—all of whom had different fathers—and Joe had a son. But that didn't discourage the two from quickly getting involved in a steamy love affair based on physical attraction and little else. Within a year, they were married.

Three months into the union, the partnership was already strained. Joe and Michelle spent the next eight years in a marriage filled with frustration, jealousy, bitter feuds, separations (often for months or years at a time), and distrust.

SEPARATE JOURNEYS

Michelle's parents divorced when she was three. She grew up in a home where "bending the truth" was acceptable, so long as the end justified the means. Michelle was engaged to a young man when she found herself pregnant as a teenager in 1965. However, her fiancé was not the father of the child. She led him to believe that baby was his—even though he wasn't the father—in order to proceed with her wedding plans. She didn't tell him the truth for twelve years (although the marriage lasted fewer than five).

During the marriage Michelle became pregnant again, but a second child didn't help solve the problem in Michelle or her husband: restlessness. Four years after they were married, Michelle's husband left her to explore what other women had to offer. But Michelle wasted no time in finding dates and moving on. She remarried a year later, in 1970.

Her second husband was a self-described hippie. Michelle easily fell into step with the free love and peace philosophy promulgated in the hippie community. She had her third child with him, but her young daughters didn't keep her from having fun with her husband, going to parties, and embracing a carefree lifestyle. As it turned out, though, marriage wasn't an institution Michelle's second husband could embrace long-term. He was a free spirit and wanted out after only two years. Michelle was fine with that.

Meanwhile, Michelle's first husband had been calling. He wanted her back. She thought, *Why not?* The two were remarried in 1973. But Michelle was still hiding the secret of her first daughter's true paternity. The deception was a strain on Michelle's ability to connect with her spouse. She found herself going out and partying with her girlfriends, and she began to realize she didn't want to be married. What she actually wanted was to have fun. It was her turn to leave him. The marriage ended in 1976.

In the mid-1970s a girlfriend invited Michelle to a Christian crusade. There she accepted Christ, or so she thought. She never followed through on the commitment she made that day. But from that point on she began wanting and seeking something—a power greater than herself.

She thought she had found that in her fourth husband. He was powerful, strong, and rich. Michelle wanted someone who could take care of her, and with him she would never have to make another decision in her life. She liked the thought of that.

They were married in 1977.

But he became controlling, domineering—and ultimately abusive. They lived in a small town in Alaska, and for stretches of time he wouldn't even let Michelle and the girls use the phone or watch television. Leaving him four years later was a tough decision because emotionally, Michelle wanted to stay. But with the safety of her children at risk, she knew she had no other option. That change brought her back to Modesto, California, her hometown. And that's when she met Joe.

By the time Joe and Michelle first locked eyes, he had racked up his share of ex-spouses as well. Like Michelle's parents, Joe's parents had split, and it had scarred him. He learned early on that being Catholic didn't necessarily stop someone from getting a divorce.

His first marriage in 1969 produced a son but ended in divorce two years later. He wanted to make it work, but they were both young and immature, and his wife had wanted out. He married again two years later, but this union didn't last much longer than the first.

About a year after his second divorce, Joe married for the third time. This union lasted longer than the other two, about five years, but ended after in-laws and business problems created a strain on the marriage.

JOE AND MICHELLE'S STORY

Soon Joe moved to Modesto, where he met his "Elizabeth Taylor."

Or that's what Michelle's family liked to call her. They saw Michelle as a beautiful, fun-loving, free spirit. With features similar to the movie star's, and a divorce count to match, her family lived vicariously through Michelle's dramatic ups and downs.

Michelle enjoyed the comparison. She was vivacious, outgoing, and energized by the high drama of her lifestyle. When she first laid eyes on Joe, she struck up a conversation with the man she thought was the spitting image of her favorite rock star, Bob Dylan.

They soon began dating. Before Joe met Michelle, he told himself he would never get involved with a woman with kids, a mistake he had made with his second marriage. But he was infatuated with Michelle. Nothing was going to get in the way of his insatiable desire to wed her. Moreover, they both thought that the lessons from their past marriages and divorces had taught them everything they needed to know to make their partnership last a lifetime. They married in 1982.

But only three months into their marriage, problems surfaced. They were in their mid-thirties and were each set in their ways. The birth of their son in 1983 didn't help matters.

Joe's vow to never again marry a woman with children seemed to be coming back to haunt him. They quickly began arguing over parenting issues. Over time, their spontaneity as a couple diminished, and the fun slowly drained from their marriage. When they fought, Joe drank, often heavily. It numbed his pain and frustration—and the looming fear that this marriage would end just as his others had.

Attributes that had once attracted Joe to Michelle in the beginning, things such as her exuberance and independence, now started to get under his skin. What's more, her ex-husbands would randomly show up to do odd jobs around the house. That really upset him. To Joe, it seemed that Michelle couldn't understand why he would be upset to see her former spouses playing handyman under his roof.

For her part, Michelle felt as if she had to walk on eggshells around Joe. She resented his drinking and considered him overly prone to unnecessary fits of jealousy. She knew she had a flirty personality and that she was something of a social butterfly, but his concerns made him seem insecure. To make matters worse, Joe would throw Michelle's past in her face when they fought. She lost respect for him, and they separated within the first year of marriage.

They tried again three months later, but the union remained rocky. Joe would take her out to dinner and buy her elaborate gifts, but he got the feeling that Michelle was ungrateful for his attention and efforts. In fact, he felt she was pretty nonchalant about him altogether. Michelle felt that Joe was putting her on a pedestal, and the feeling was smothering her.

They separated again in 1985, this time for eight months. During that period, Michelle rededicated her life to Christ. Joe ended up doing the same. But Michelle was dubious of his motives, wondering if he was merely trying to trick her back into the marriage. When Joe continued to show up for church each Sunday, she gave him the benefit of the doubt. She began to wonder if a so-called "Christian marriage" was the answer to keeping a partnership solid and unbreakable. They gave it another go, even renewing their vows.

The honeymoon didn't last long. All the same problems remained, though Joe's drinking was no longer an issue. Nevertheless, the two were unable to resolve their conflicts. Their verbal arguments were as ferocious as ever. They fought over everything, from bank accounts to dinner menus.

Michelle was raised in a family that held nothing back when expressing anger. She was accustomed to cussing, hitting, and throwing things in an argument. Joe was the target of her frustration and rage. So even with attending church regularly and going to Bible studies, their happy front was a façade. It became too much for them to bear. They separated—again—in 1987.

The Turnaround

In the past, during their fights and separations Michelle's focus had been solely on Joe—what he was doing wrong, his faults and problems. In former attempts to revive their marriage, the two had put the emphasis on couples therapy and counseling. But this time, the split was different. Since they knew from past experience that their own efforts could not make the relationship work, they felt they had no choice but to move forward alone with no hope of reconciliation.

Instead, they individually came to the end of themselves and turned to Christ. Without knowing the other was doing so, they each began focusing on strengthening their relationship with the Lord. Michelle began to spend time with other Christian women and to study what it meant to be a "godly wife"—even though she was living without her husband. And Joe let go of his obsession with Michelle and began spending time with other Christian men. He began to realize he had a lot in common with them. Their camaraderie filled a void in Joe that he didn't know he had.

Joe and Michelle each began to understand their own personality flaws and see that in many ways they had been acting selfishly. Separately, but simultaneously, a sense of personal responsibility grew within them. They began letting go of their unrealistic expectations of one another. The growth in their faith also helped them begin to realize the destructive nature of their angry outbursts and disrespectful attitudes.

At one point, when Joe thought Michelle might move back to Alaska, he finally came to understand that he could not rely on her for his happiness, and he finally turned his faith and trust completely toward Jesus Christ for fulfillment. Joe's time alone, and in praying with other men and reading the Bible, caused him to put Jesus first and Michelle second. Joe's new outlook on life gave him more confidence and allowed him to relax.

Michelle was surprised to see Joe making good decisions for himself, and she started to realize that he didn't need her anymore. That was when she started yearning for him again. Her respect for and attraction to him was restored. She could finally breathe around him, and Joe felt comfortable being himself around her. Two years after the separation, they recommitted their lives to each other.

THE MINISTRY

One year later, they started a marriage ministry. It is a ministry based on the notion of fixing yourself instead of fixing your spouse. The effort has exponentially expanded over the last seventeen years. Joe and Michelle know that their own "colorful" history is what makes them perfect for marital counseling. For them, it's not necessarily about book smarts but street smarts—and the wisdom that comes from seeking God daily. They have "been there, done that" and can truly relate with every couple they meet.

When men assume that Joe can't understand their plight, because they are going on their second or third divorce, Joe simply smiles and listens, and then assures them that he can, indeed, understand what they must be thinking and feeling.

Michelle also believes that her life choices have enabled her to successfully minister to other women. But she does have one huge regret: what she put her children through. They suffered through it all and continue to reap the ramifications to this day in different ways. It pains Michelle greatly to know that she is a major cause of that.

The Williams' marriage hasn't been 100 percent smooth sailing over the last seventeen years. Michelle's four children have four different fathers, and that has caused some tension. But to Joe and Michelle, life is now a series of issues they must give up to God. They tell couples that if they try to run their own lives instead of giving them to God, they are in for trouble and heartache. They advise that throwing around the "D-word" (divorce) only greatly exacerbates things. That is not to say they don't support the notion of separation, if necessary, but filing for divorce is another matter. Commitment is about getting through anything and everything together.

They urge married couples to be quick to forgive, to accept their spouse for who he or she is, to not complain about their spouse to others, to always make it a point to spend time alone with God in prayer, and to maintain an emotional support system.

Marriage isn't only about one person's happiness. And it's not something in which the other person is there to make you happy. A good marriage is one in which both the husband and wife can have fun, feel safe, and be themselves. Joe and Michelle encourage couples to put Jesus Christ first and their spouse second. Joe even wears two wedding bands to illustrate that point.

Putting together the pieces of a broken marriage doesn't happen overnight. In Joe and Michelle's case, it took several years. But in the end, they reconciled. They like to say they finally found success when they did it God's way.

—*As told to Jennifer Kabbany Dawson*

$\infty \bullet \infty$

Joe and Michelle Williams are the founders of The International Center for Reconciling God's Way, Inc., a faith-based, nonprofit ministry in Modesto, California. The ministry provides help and resources for troubled marriages and equips pastors and leaders to begin "Marriage 911" ministries for crisis and separated couples in their church and community.

Joe and Michelle also recently authored the book *Yes, Your Marriage Can Be Saved*, published by Focus on the Family and Tyndale House. Various churches offering "Reconciling God's Way" and "Marriage 911" classes are listed on their Web site.

The International Center for Reconciling God's Way
Joe and Michelle Williams
(800) 205-6808
www.reconcilinggodsway.org
reconcile@reconcilinggodsway.org

> *"Saying you're sorry is relatively easy. Asking for forgiveness is more difficult. You are allowing the other person to make the choice to forgive you. You are giving them the power to say yes or no."*

RON'S STORY

Ron Anderson found himself in a most uncomfortable position, a situation unlike anything he had imagined he would ever face. After all, no young husband ever daydreams about picking up the phone and speaking to the man his wife has been having an affair with. But Ron found himself doing just that on an emotional afternoon in 1980.

Just a few hours earlier, Ron had been attending a business convention in town, but his mind had been elsewhere. As hard as he had tried to focus, he simply couldn't make himself concentrate. The events of his personal life were vastly overshadowing the events of the convention, so he left early and headed home. As he walked through the door of the condominium, he was greeted by a sight he hadn't seen in weeks: his wife. Nancy was sitting on their couch, in the dark, alone.

She's come home, he thought. *Everything is going to be okay.*

There *was* hope, initially. It seemed as if Nancy had returned from their separation ready to begin life anew. Four weeks earlier, he had begged her not to leave, promising to stop the yelling, pledging to be a better husband, and even suggesting a renewed focus on their spiritual lives. The marriage had been strained; he knew that. Still, he'd been blindsided when she had announced she was moving out. He had pleaded with her to reconsider.

"You make me miserable," had been Nancy's devastating response. She had picked up her suitcase and defiantly walked out the door. Soon after, she informed Ron of her intention to file for divorce.

When he had heard that word—*divorce*—the magnitude of the situation had begun to set in. The thought of losing Nancy forever had been overwhelming, leaving Ron an emotional wreck. He sought answers from friends and family, but they had no answers to give.

Now he had returned home to find her sitting on their sofa, awaiting his arrival. *Maybe the situation will resolve itself easily*, Ron thought. *This time apart has been only a few weeks out of the two years we have been married. I can be a better husband, and we can be happy.* He even had hope that his worst fear—which yet remained unspoken—was unfounded.

That thin sliver of hope dissolved quickly.

"I've been lying to you for months," Nancy told him. She confessed that she had moved out for reasons other than just her unhappiness. The fighting and constant cycle of disappointment had only been part of her reasoning. Nancy revealed that there was another man in her life. His name was Jake, and he was a co-worker. They had been seeing each other for months, and she loved him. Jake made her feel special, she said. He treated her as she wanted to be treated. He was everything to her that Ron had failed to be.

The news was painful to hear, but Ron appreciated the honesty. The desire to fix his marriage outweighed the pain of the admitted affair. As they talked, the initial hope of an easy reconciliation was replaced by a different hope. Now that they were finally communicating honestly, perhaps there was hope they could achieve a fundamental change in their relationship.

NANCY'S STORY

For her part, Nancy found it hard to believe she was even talking to Ron. Just a few hours earlier, seeing her husband was the least appealing thing she could think of. Thinking that Ron was out of town, Nancy had taken the opportunity to return to the condo to retrieve some personal belongings. She had no intention of being there when Ron returned, but before she could leave, the phone rang.

It was her mother.

Over the previous weeks, Nancy had successfully hidden her separation from her parents. They lived across the country, which made it easy to hide the truth from them — at least for a while. Nancy was reluctant to tell them about her problems. They were religious people with a strong belief in the institution of marriage, and Nancy knew they would be disappointed in her if they found out she had left Ron.

Answering that phone call changed everything. At first, Nancy tried to cover her situation, insisting to her mother that she was fine. She was there at home to answer the phone, after all. Even when her mother revealed that she had awoken in the night with a deep conviction that her daughter was in trouble, Nancy clung to her feeble story. It wasn't until her father came on the line that her alibi broke down. Nancy had never been able to lie to her father, and this time was no different. When he asked, Nancy had to admit that all was not well in her marriage.

As she told her parents the story, they questioned her motives. Had Ron ever hit her? Had he cheated on her? Had he done anything so severe that it justified breaking the holy bond of matrimony? Was there any good reason to toss aside the vow of a man and woman standing before God and pledging their intent to remain together for the rest of their lives? The answer to all of those questions was no.

Nancy's mother waited for a long time — long enough to pray for guidance — and then said, "Nancy, we love you. And because we love you, we will not support your leaving Ron. You would be outside of God's will if you ended your marriage."

The thought of God's will having any bearing on her life further weakened Nancy's already failing sense of bravado. She hadn't thought about God in months. The only thing of importance had been her devotion to Jake and her determination to end her marriage to be with him. Ron had become an obstacle to her. Her marriage was an inconvenience that could be trounced. She had moved out with no real intention of returning.

"I haven't been a good wife," she admitted.

"But that can change," her father replied.

Her parents reconfirmed their love for her and offered to pray with her before hanging up. Nancy listened to the prayer that petitioned God to help Ron and Nancy restore their marriage. While she had begun to see the injustice of her own actions, Nancy wasn't convinced that she really wanted the outcome her father prayed for. But she agreed to wait for Ron to return and promised to call her parents the next morning.

As she waited, she felt the prayer begin to soften her heart. She began to cry tears of sadness and grief for the pain she had caused and the pain she had endured. She wanted to turn the chaos of her world into a peaceful, ordered life, but she could see no means of accomplishing such a mighty deed.

Nancy prayed for guidance, surrendering to the truth of her parents' words. From the prayerful phone call to her own pleading with God to help her understand what path she should take, Nancy found the wall of guilt and shame she had erected slowly melting away. Suddenly she was reminded of the words Jesus had spoken to an adulterous woman: "Go, and sin no more." In that moment, she knew what she had to do. She waited for her husband to come home.

Though she spoke calmly to Ron and admitted her mistakes with great candor, Nancy wasn't emotionally convinced to do what she rationally knew must be done. She loved Jake, and at that moment she couldn't say the same about her husband.

What she was thinking about doing would shatter her heart and Jake's. They had discussed their future together, making secret plans as secret lovers do. Jake planned to leave his wife and children to be with her. Together, they believed they would find a fulfillment of everything lacking in their current marriages. Nancy was emotionally bonded with Jake in a way she had not experienced with Ron. The thought of giving that up was unbearable.

Nancy forced the words out of her mouth. Even though it broke her heart to say it, she told Ron that she would break up with Jake and quit her job so she would never see him again. She told Ron she was sorry for the hurt she had caused.

Nancy's decision brought them to the most awkward of moments: breaking up with Jake.

THE PHONE CALL

They called Jake together. Nancy spoke to Jake first, telling him she would not see him anymore and explaining why she would not be coming back to work. Weeping as she spoke, Nancy also told Jake that she hoped he would restore his own broken family as she was attempting to do. Then Ron took the phone and spoke to the man his wife had been having an affair with, asking him to never contact her again. Jake tearfully agreed to honor Ron's request.

With that phone call, one chapter in Ron and Nancy Anderson's life had ended, but there were many more to be written.

They moved forward. Ron made an effort to be a better husband, and Nancy began to sort through the complex web of lies and self-deception she had created. But there was something missing, and it was identified by Nancy's father during a family visit.

REBUILDING

Nancy's father, Richard, asked Ron if the couple had figured out how their marriage had been broken and if they had a plan to fix it.

"I don't want to talk about what she did," Ron admitted. "It's too painful. Nancy is home. We'll just move on from here."

But Richard told him it wasn't that simple. "If you rebuild a house on a cracked foundation," he said, "it might be all right for a while, but when storms come, your house will be torn apart."

During the discussion, Ron divulged that while Nancy had apologized for her indiscretion, she had not asked for his forgiveness.

"Nancy," her father said to her, "when you tell someone you are sorry, that is *your* choice. Saying you're sorry is relatively easy. Asking for forgiveness is more difficult. You are allowing the other person to make the choice to forgive you. You are giving them the power to say yes or no."

Then he turned to Ron. "The responsibility doesn't just rest on the one asking for forgiveness. If you decide to forgive Nancy, you can never use her sin against her. If you choose not to forgive—if you want to hold on to the pain or to try to punish her—I don't think you'll stay married. It will be your decision, but you'll have to accept the consequences of your choice."

After a long, restless night, Nancy came to terms with the lesson her father had lovingly taught her. The next morning, she decided to ask Ron for forgiveness. "Ron, I've betrayed you. I've lied to you and deceived you. I have no defense. Can you, will you, please forgive me?"

Ron took Nancy's hands in his. There was no doubt about what he wanted to do. "Nancy, we have both done and said terrible things. Our marriage was a mess, and a lot of it was my fault. Even though you betrayed me, I choose to forgive you."

While the decision to forgive came easily, the rebuilding of their marriage took a long time. Ron and Nancy had to work through many more issues before their marriage would feel whole again. They found it easy to slip back into old patterns and had to consciously remind themselves to be more caring and loving. Nancy struggled to forgive herself and to put past mistakes behind her. Some weeks it was all they could do to be civil to each other. Other weeks were filled with a renewed love, which began to drive out the familiar patterns of hurt and hostility. Gradually, the good weeks began to outnumber the bad.

Through it all, they attempted to offer each other mercy when they slipped up. The key was to recognize in each other the desire to change and avoid overreacting when the other partner failed to demonstrate proper care or consideration. It was one of the harder habits to break. In the past, they were each waiting for the other to slip up, ready to criticize even the tiniest mistake. Now, they attempted to exercise self-control and patience. Instead of looking back at past failures, they chose to focus on the pure, admirable, lovely, and good things they desired in their marriage.

Even before these positive characteristics were visible, the Andersons were able to look ahead and visualize the beautiful thing their marriage could become. Keeping that in mind helped them focus their energy on reaching the goal.

Through it all, they had help. Nancy's parents were an ongoing source of encouragement and example. Ron and Nancy attended marriage counseling and renewed their focus on their spiritual lives. They got involved in a marriage group at church, looking to other strong couples for guidance and support. They were able to tap into the resources around them to help bolster their efforts and solidify their foundation.

During this time, Ron learned a key lesson in his development as a husband. After reading a particular Scripture passage, he came to realize he was called to try to understand his wife. Like most husbands, Ron found it easy to dismiss Nancy's feelings and actions. Things that were unfamiliar or irrational to him were part of her "being a woman." It was as if she had an incurable disease.

This attitude had been a contributing factor in the breakdown of their marriage. His lack of understanding had alienated Nancy, leaving the door open for her to seek understanding elsewhere. When he began to try to understand the thought processes and differences between the genders, he was able to more fully appreciate his wife and meet her needs.

Together Ron and Nancy began to understand and celebrate their differences in a way that brought them closer together. They began to demonstrate new levels of respect and appreciation for one another through compliments and encouragement. They were careful not to take each other for granted, and they always looked for areas of self-improvement.

And though it was a slow process, the efforts paid off. Now, more than twenty-five years after Nancy's affair, the Andersons' marriage is vibrantly restored and stronger than ever.

—*Eric S. Wyatt*

Nancy C. Anderson is the author of *Avoiding the Greener Grass Syndrome.* In this book, she encourages spouses to water the grass on his or her own side of the fence and to build hedges around their own relationship.

Nancy is also a nationally known speaker. Her talks and seminars are helpful for couples restored after infidelity and for those simply seeking to build better relational skills. She often speaks at couples' seminars and women's retreats.

Nancy C. Anderson
P. O. Box 4396
Huntington Beach, CA 92605
(714) 206-9540
www.nancycanderson.com
ncawrites@msn.com

One of my greatest fears was that Tom would leave me, yet my hysterical clinging could have actually made this a reality. We were reacting to one another out of our fear and creating a painful power struggle for each other.

BEV

The Chicago wind blew through me, cutting me like a knife, as I walked through the campus of Northern Illinois University, where I attended graduate school. Tom and I had been married only six months when he moved us away from balmy Los Angeles. I loved L.A. with its palm trees and constant summer breeze. But, as the dutiful wife, I traded it all to follow Tom to the dreaded frigidity of Illinois when he took a job at a college there. This was just one in a long line of resentments that had begun to brew in my soul as a young bride.

I hated the cold weather. I grew up in the South, where it rarely snowed. And when it *did* snow, it was a glorious occasion. Schools closed, and work was canceled. It was a time for snowmen, sleds, and eating snow cream. The North was a different story. When it snowed there, they didn't close anything. They marched on through the frozen stuff.

Don't get me wrong; the first Chicago snowfall was beautiful with its stunning white powder covering the landscape. Pine trees looked like crystal angels. Elms and maples wore icy shawls to outline their silhouettes. It was magical. But then the snow stayed and stayed and stayed. As the weather grew colder, my heart cooled with it. But I shoved my pain and resentment down deep in my soul, afraid to make waves.

My parents had fought constantly and finally divorced, so I had concluded that fighting led straight to divorce. I had vowed to never fight in my marriage. I avoided conflict at all costs. I believed that by doing so I was merely being a godly wife— practicing a gentle, quiet spirit, as the Bible talks about in 1 Peter 3:4.

That's what I believed. What I know now is that withdrawal and stonewalling are the highest predictors of divorce in America.

But what did I know back then? I was twenty-two years old and fresh out of an extremely dysfunctional family. My childhood had left me without any kind of model to follow in building a healthy marriage. Tom's situation was not much better. His parents had divorced after twenty-five years of struggle. As children of divorce, both of us felt like fish out of water when dealing with marital conflict.

Our parents' divorces were not the only demons in our newly formed marriage. As a child, I had endured severe physical and verbal abuse at the hands of a mentally ill mother. Similarly, Tom's father was critical, negative, and impossible to please. These scars set us up for difficulty in "doing marriage" successfully.

As I walked along the frozen tundra of a campus, my soul was heavy, remembering the awful fight Tom and I had just the night before. While the snow pummeled my face, the bitter memory pounded on my heart.

That night I had been so proud of myself as I prepared dinner for my new groom. We were poor and living from paycheck to paycheck, so I had prepared a delicious, nutritious dinner for only $1.88. The Proverbs 31 woman had nothing on me! I thought I was truly the ideal bride. But that economical meal happened to be quiche. Unfortunately, a book came out in the early 1970s that quickly became a thorn in my side—*Real Men Don't Eat Quiche.* I want to find this clever author someday and tell him the trouble his "literary contribution" caused my marriage early on.

As I prepared the food, Tom began making faces, curling his lip, and asking what I put in the quiche. He then informed me of his distaste for mushy egg dishes.

Now, as he tells the story in workshops, he says that this had nothing to do with him being a "real man" at all. His honest impression of quiche is that it looks like something that has been eaten once, brought back up, baked, and served again. Usually this gets a *yuck* response from the audience, which further proves his point.

As we sat at the kitchen table "discussing" quiche, our conversation quickly turned into an argument. Tom got heated and announced, "I'm leaving. I'm going to go out on the porch to cool off."

When he was young, his mother told him that all good, hot-blooded, Portuguese boys should cool off when they get mad. He was taught that, in lieu of losing his temper and hurting someone's feelings, he should instead go outside and calm down. One would think that I, his bride, would see the healthy rationale in this—but no! To my surprise, I had a *major* meltdown as he stood to leave.

"Leave! Did I hear you say *leave?*" I cried hysterically. I clung to his leg. "Pleeeease don't leave! How could you be so mean as to leave me at a time like this?"

"Huh?" He was incredulous. "What are you so upset about? I'm just cooling off like my mom taught me years ago! Can't a guy get a break around here?" At that moment Tom thought he had married a psycho woman.

What was worse, I thought I had become one! What had happened to our wonderful honeymoon haven? Why did we both feel so raw, so betrayed? These questions troubled me as I made the icy trek to school.

When I arrived at my professor's office for our weekly consultation, I was so frozen I didn't remove my hat, coat, or gloves. As you can imagine, Professor Jones gave me a curious look. Cold, to me, was forty degrees. Cold, to him, was forty below.

I could hardly contain myself as I sat before my wise mentor. "Boy, do I have a story for you," I said, barely holding back the tears. He could tell I was about to replay another difficult scene from my young marriage. I spilled the whole sordid quiche affair.

He listened intently; then he addressed me calmly. "I'm going to give you a preview of the neurobiology unit I will be teaching next semester."

I wasn't sure what neurobiology had to do with my marriage, but I was about to find out.

"Brain function has a great deal to do with how we respond to real or perceived pain." I sniffed back the tears, grabbed my notepad, as I had done many times before, and tried not to miss a word.

"Humans are the only mammals that have a *new* brain," he said, as he stroked his Freudian-like beard. "The *new* brain is the part of the brain that helps us take in information, organize it, and make decisions. It gives us the ability to observe ourselves and evaluate our own behavior.

"Beneath the new brain lies the brain stem, or *old* brain. Cradled at the root of the brain stem is the limbic system, which is our survival mechanism. This primitive old brain is a part of our fight-or-flight response. It floods our body with chemicals when it senses fear or danger. Painful memories from childhood can trigger the old brain's fight-or-flight response."

Wow, this is making sense to me, I thought. Off came the hat and gloves. I was writing profusely.

Seeing the light bulb go on in my head, he continued. "When our autonomic nervous system kicks in, we have physiological triggers, such as sweaty palms, heart palpitations, panic, and perspiration. Another key aspect of the old brain is that it has no sense of time. So a trauma that occurred at age five can be relived at age twenty-five, with the same feelings and emotions that you felt as a child."

"What?" I said. "You mean that last night I was responding to a wound that happened in my childhood?" I shrugged my coat off my shoulders in a writing frenzy.

"Yes," he said. "In psychology, we call this *reactivity*. We are *reactive* when we give a present-day situation more emotion than it deserves because it has triggered a childhood soul wound."

"You mean I'm not crazy?" I asked, heaving a huge sigh of relief, unable to hold back a floodgate of tears.

"No, you are not crazy, just reactive."

As tears rolled down my cheeks, I was lost in thought, remembering a painful memory from my childhood that I thought I had carefully buried years ago.

As a young girl, I became anxious and fearful when my parents fought, because the conflicts often resulted in violence. My father frequently threatened to leave my mother, but he never followed through. Then one night, when I was five years old, they had a particularly bad fight. And this time when my father said he was leaving, somehow I knew he meant it. He told my mother that he couldn't take her wild antics anymore. I knew that my mother was not normal. She said and did crazy, violent things, and I panicked at the thought of being left alone with her, having to take care of my younger brother and sister. I feared for our safety.

In sheer terror, I grabbed hold of my father's leg and clung to it for dear life. I begged and pleaded with him to stay. Exasperated, he dragged me across the plank floor, opened the screen to the porch, and slung me off, saying, "Sorry, kiddo. I'm outta here." I embedded my fingernails in the screen door and begged for my father to come back. But he just kept walking.

I had done everything in my power to put this painful memory out of my mind. And I'd been successful, until that night with the quiche. Unfortunately, my reactivity had triggered a similar soul wound in Tom, and he became reactive as well.

TOM

I grew up in a Christian home and had a pretty good childhood. But when I was thirteen years old, I discovered that my father was having an affair with a nurse at our family doctor's office. When I told my mom the horrible news, it blew our family apart. Mom and Dad just barely managed to stick it out for the next ten years, but they were never close again.

In her pain, my mom began confiding in me and frequently told me what a poor Christian and bad husband my father was. I wanted to be there for her, but her constant clinging and neediness were suffocating me. I was anxious to graduate high school and go off to college just to get away from her constant smothering. I, like Bev, thought I could outrun those painful feeling of being clung to . . . until the "quiche affair."

That night, as I stood up to leave the room and cool off, Bev reacted to her childhood soul wound of abandonment by begging, clinging, and pleading for me to return. Unfortunately, her reaction triggered my soul wound of being emotionally suffocated by my mom. I overreacted and felt the overwhelming urge to escape. Bev's reactivity triggered *my* reactivity, and both of us severely overreacted.

Psychologists now call this phenomenon *interactivity.* But back then, we just knew it as marital purgatory. We were wounding each other in much the same way our parents had wounded us, and we could not seem to stop.

BEV

One of my greatest fears was that Tom would leave me, yet my hysterical clinging could have actually made this a reality. My reactivity could have made it difficult for him to stay. We were doing that which we hated, because we were reacting out of our fear and creating a painful power struggle for each other. It truly *was* marital purgatory.

Professor Jones told me that the psychological cure for reactivity was *intentionality*. Intentionality is a concept used a great deal in self-help groups involving addiction. "Fake it 'til you make it," they say. In other words, act a certain way regardless of what you are feeling, and eventually the correct feelings will follow.

Alcoholics Anonymous teaches that even if you do not feel like walking past the bar door—and you're dying to go inside for a drink—walk on past the door anyway. After awhile, your feelings will follow your behavior. Many AA participants refer to this as "white-knuckle sobriety." This means staying sober by an act of your will, not your emotions. When it comes to marital fidelity, we call it "white-knuckle matrimony."

After meeting with my professor that day, I drove the thirty miles home from school practically bursting with new information. I was eager to tell Tom all I had learned so that we could develop a plan to move out of our marital purgatory and into a place of health. As I drove past the sleeping cornfields and mounds of gray snow, I thought to myself, *Perhaps this frost will end inside and outside of my life, and spring will come again after all.*

I rushed into our small apartment, dropped my books on the floor, and plopped into the cushy beanbag chair that was the sole piece of furniture in our new love nest. (I told you we were poor.) Tom sat across from me on a pile of pillows, and I poured out all the wisdom I had gained that day. We then sat there looking at each other, kind of stuck, trying to figure out how we were going to become intentional.

In our psychology classes, we had learned that if you act a certain way, feelings will follow. As aspiring therapists, this made sense to us. But we wondered where we were going to get the emotional strength, moral fortitude, or desire to act loving when we felt that our own needs were not being met. Try as we might, Tom and I could not imagine being intentional and calm when our childhood soul wounds were being triggered. We both knew that when we reacted, we seemed to lose control of our actions.

One problem we encountered with this new information was that it did not completely align with our core beliefs. Thirty years ago, psychology was approached from a purely human perspective. Christian counseling was almost nonexistent. As pioneers in the field, we had to take what we could get and integrate our faith into what we were learning. Humanistic psychology teaches that man is basically good and he can be intentional by an act of his will. The Bible teaches that man is sinful and in need of God's redemption. Tom and I knew that we were weak, fleshly creatures who could not practice intentionality on our own.

Then it hit us. In the marriage relationship, intentionality is pure *agape*, which means loving unconditionally no matter how you are treated. Agape acts loving even when it is being wounded. Suddenly, Tom and I had a simultaneous revelation: this is exactly what Jesus did on the cross for us. He loved the very people who were putting Him to death. And God continues to give His children unconditional love. His gift cannot be earned and is not deserved, yet He still chooses to give it.

So, if we act loving and healing when we are hurting, we will be like Jesus. What, then, can motivate us to act intentionally or with agape? Certainly not our basic, innate goodness. It is the example of Jesus' unconditional love for us that enables us to give agape love to our mate, even when we are wounded and don't feel like it. Because He loved us unconditionally when we were wounding Him by our sin, we can love each other when we are being wounded. It is His strength, not our will, that makes this possible.

That night began our journey of turning soul-wounding moments into soul-healing moments, and we're still doing it more than three decades later. It was also the beginning of a model of marital therapy called Soul-Healing Love, a model we have used with thousands of couples over the past twenty-seven years in our counseling clinic. We now teach this model across the globe and continue to do Soul Healers Couples Intensive Weekends, in which we share with couples what we learned so many years ago. We have written books and developed training products that also enhance our ministry.

We have often said that we want to take our last breath in the counseling chair helping another couple "get it." We believe that this is what the Lord put us on the planet to accomplish, and today there is no greater joy for either of us.

By the way, we did finally move from the frigid wilderness of Illinois to the gorgeous green grass of North Carolina—and that did wonders for our relationship too. After twenty-seven years in this warm southern climate, I think I have finally thawed out!

—Dr. Beverly and Dr. Tom Rodgers

Doctors Beverly and Tom Rodgers are the founders and co-directors of the Institute for Soul Healing Love. They are authors of *Soul Healing Love* and several other books focused on forming healthy relationships.

Their Soul Healing Love model explores how childhood

wounds can affect our adult relationships, and it provides methods for individuals and families to begin healing. Bev and Tom speak worldwide and provide whole-person Christian counseling for a full range of issues. They also offer workshops for couples, singles, and church leaders.

The Institute for Soul Healing Love
Doctors Beverly and Tom Rodgers
1206 Jules Court
Charlotte, NC 28226
(704) 364-9176
www.soulhealinglove.com
info@soulhealinglove.com

Being young and in love wasn't enough for Scott and Cathy to make a perfect life together. "I was a fighter, and Scott swept things under the rug," Cathy says. "We rarely dealt with the issues."

When Scott and Cathy first locked eyes in college in the late 1980s, there was an immediate and mutual spark between them. Scott, a sophomore at Indiana's Ball State University, was helping freshmen move into the dorms. Cathy was among the newcomers. When Scott first laid eyes on her, he was struck by her beauty and engaging smile. Cathy thought Scott seemed more mature than the other guys on campus and was impressed. But it wasn't meant to be just yet. Scott already had a girlfriend, and Cathy had a boyfriend.

The following year, the two ended up in the same coed dorm and frequently planned student gatherings together. "While working together we became more attracted to each other," Cathy says. They soon discovered they had other things in common. Both were raised in small Indiana towns by old-fashioned parents who didn't believe in divorce and who raised their children to have a strong moral compass.

After some time spent as friends, they started dating. Scott broke up with his former girlfriend to begin a relationship with Cathy. "Cathy was full of energy," he says with a smile. "She was outgoing and never missed an opportunity to be the center of attention." Scott considered himself reserved, quiet, and laid-back, and he was attracted to qualities in Cathy that he lacked.

Cathy saw something special in Scott as well. Every time their eyes met, she felt her knees tremble. "He could melt my heart with one look," Cathy says now. They continued dating throughout college, nurturing the notion that they were meant for each other.

After they had been dating for about three years, they went on a short drive to Cathy's parents' house for dinner. Scott stopped for gas and, with a gleam in his eye, asked Cathy to reach into the glove compartment for something. She pulled out a huge diamond engagement ring.

Cathy had been waiting for this moment for months, but she says, "I was caught by surprise. I didn't expect it to happen at a gas station!" Still, she couldn't say yes fast enough. The summer after Cathy graduated, they got married. The August 1991 ceremony included all the bells and whistles of a fairytale wedding, including 450 guests and a billowy champagne-pink gown with a long train. They even wrote their own vows.

"Life was good," Cathy says. "We were madly in love."

The Honeymoon Is Over

But as it turned out, being young and in love wasn't enough for Scott and Cathy to make a perfect life together. "As conflicts arose," Cathy says, "I was a fighter, and Scott swept things under the rug. We rarely dealt with the issues."

Once they settled into their new home, Scott continued in his position as a marketing representative for a major oil company —a job that demanded long hours and frequent out-of-town trips. Cathy took a retail job at a local mall, but she didn't make any real friends there. "I was living in a town where I knew no one. I was a complete scaredy-cat—terrified to be alone overnight. So when he was gone, I was miserable."

Cathy began to complain to Scott about her situation, and he grew weary of her constant nagging. They had been married less than a year, but Cathy began to second-guess her decision to marry Scott.

Later that year, Cathy became a Christian. "I felt more alive," Cathy says, "but I still felt alone. The couple who led me to the Lord lived far away, in Arizona, and Scott did not have a personal relationship with Christ."

Before long, Scott was offered a transfer, and the couple moved to his hometown. Scott says that around this time, "My best friend, Dave, shared with me his testimony of *thinking* he was a Christian all of his life. He said that it wasn't until he began to struggle with sin in his marriage that he realized that he had never chosen a personal relationship with Christ. His words just spoke to me." Soon Scott became a Christian as well. Together, Scott and Cathy joined a local church, got involved in Bible studies, and began volunteering in their community.

The couple finally seemed to find their groove. Scott changed jobs again, becoming vice president of petroleum for a convenience store chain. Between making new friends at church, working, and keeping busy at home, their marriage stabilized. "Compared to what we knew or ever had as a married couple," Cathy says, "it was better — even good. But it was still not what we had hoped for."

In Different Worlds

Then came their first child. Cathy devoted herself entirely to her daughter and became a stay-at-home mom. Meanwhile, Scott threw himself into his job, maintaining seventy-hour work weeks. "My job was my priority and took all my energy. I was mentally and physically exhausted from making decisions all day, and when I got home I was spent."

But somehow he managed to find time to take business calls at home. That really got under Cathy's skin. "It hurt to hear him talking with the people at work when I felt he never really engaged in conversation with me."

Cathy says she loved being a stay-at-home wife and mom, "but physically, mentally, and emotionally, I was overwhelmed. I prayed for a better marriage. I read all the right books. I tried to make the relationship different." But eventually she became indifferent about her relationship with Scott. "We coexisted. Anything I was involved in, he had no part in." She couldn't imagine things getting any better.

Within a few years, the couple had two more children, but there was no change in their relationship. "Many times I tried to share with him how I was feeling emotionally," Cathy says, "but for some reason he just didn't see how his lack of balance between work and home was destroying our family."

When Scott *was* at home, he drifted around in a fog, just going through the motions. And Cathy found herself overwhelmed with responsibilities. "I didn't feel like Scott was on my team. I knew I didn't bring any money to the household, but I contributed in plenty of other ways—very important ways. I was the disciplinarian, the spiritual leader, the cook, the maid, and everything else my home and family demanded. Whenever I was spiritually strong I could carry the load, but when I became weaker Satan got a foothold."

With no hope of change in sight, Cathy's resentment toward Scott grew. "I was just finished trying for a better marriage. I was beaten down and broken, and I had nothing left."

Scott took on more responsibilities at work. He didn't know what Cathy was going through, nor did he really ask. He began making poor choices about financial issues and kept Cathy isolated from his daily decision making. Their communication didn't go beyond mundane small talk, and yet Scott didn't see a problem with the way things were.

"I was just clueless," he says now. "It was like I was on a different planet." Cathy voiced her frustrations here and there, but he wasn't hearing her. He was too busy keeping his head above water at work. "Since we didn't have a strong foundation in our relationship, I didn't feel comfortable opening up to her—I didn't even know how to, because I was unclear what a healthy relationship looked like. Since our relationship with God through Christ had ceased to be important to us anymore, our relationship with each other wasn't important either."

Soon, they left their church. "We began 'church-hopping,' and my walk with the Lord became weaker and weaker every day," Cathy explains. "As Satan distracted me, I started to crumble. He convinced me that I couldn't live life this way any longer, and I would be happier not being married to Scott. I started to plan how I would get out of all of this. But to Scott and all of my friends, I played the 'everything is fine' game."

In 2002, it all came crashing down. "I had hurt my hand and needed to see a physical therapist," Cathy says. The therapist was kind, and Cathy found herself growing attracted to him. "During the sessions, we would talk about our lives and interests. I was taken aback by this guy who was so much like me. It felt good to talk with someone who actually listened and remembered the things I said. This guy felt like my soul mate."

What had started as an innocent friendship soon developed into much more. She couldn't wait to get to her "appointments," and the relationship with the therapist soon progressed beyond mere friendship.

Even so, the affair was bittersweet. "I can remember a battle going on between my flesh and my soul. Feeding my flesh felt very good. But my soul was hurting and crying out."

A WAKE-UP CALL

One day Cathy let Scott have it. "I was brutally honest with Scott about how I felt," she says. "I told him I was done and didn't love him anymore and everything about him sickened me. I told him he could try to win me back, but I was making plans to leave."

Scott was floored. He had never heard her say things like that before. With her words, reality struck him between the eyes. His life was completely out of balance.

Scott immediately began to change. Right away, he says, "God put it on my heart that my relationship with Him wasn't right. And I wasn't treating Cathy like the bride of Christ. As a result, every thought and action soon became all about Cathy. She would tell you I was so attentive to her that I quickly smothered her, but I was ashamed for how I had neglected her."

A few weeks later, he began to notice that Cathy's stories about where she was and what she was doing didn't add up. One day he flat-out asked her if there was someone else. She finally admitted it.

Though he was heartbroken, Scott decided to take personal responsibility for neglecting Cathy and pushing her away from him and eventually over the edge. "What I didn't know at the time," Scott explains, "is that taking personal responsibility is the number one factor in predicting success for a marriage in crisis." He humbled himself and asked God to change the man he had become. He began waking before dawn to pray for his family and his relationship with his wife.

But Cathy was through. She could barely stand the sight of Scott. When he asked her questions, she would answer them with harsh candor. "I lived in pure hell as I tried to satisfy the flesh rather than live under God's rule," Cathy says.

A Last Resort

They had been emotionally estranged for about eight months when Scott asked her to go with him to an intensive marital counseling retreat at the National Institute of Marriage in Branson, Missouri. She begrudgingly agreed, if only to get Scott off her back. Cathy thought maybe he would finally leave her alone after she went along with this.

The retreat was not what they had expected. "It was not a 'quick fix' for your marriage," says Cathy, reflecting on the experience. "This was a time to heal. God met me and started working and wooing me back in small, subtle ways. We learned great tools to help us communicate in a healthy, real, loving way. Brick by brick my wall with Scott started coming down."

Afterward she ended the affair. Slowly she came around to the idea that maybe her marriage was worth saving.

She couldn't blame Scott for the affair. It was, after all, her choice. But she had suffered from a lack of love and affection in her marriage. "To his credit, Scott took personal responsibility for not 'being there' as a husband," Cathy says. "The fact that he never threw the affair in my face helped us both heal and move on more quickly. Scott definitely went the extra mile — not me."

The couple slowly began applying some of the principles they had learned at the retreat — principles such as healing yourself physically, mentally, and spiritually before trying to fix your relationship; putting a relationship with God above all else; and carving out personal time to relax and center yourself.

Scott stopped smothering Cathy — stopped trying so hard to fix all their problems himself. "God gave me a peace that He was in control," Scott explains. "I had gotten to a point where I realized there was nothing I could do to change Cathy. Only He could do that. I decided to just back off and let God work. And did He work!"

Scott also quit his job. "It got to the point that if I really wanted to change, I had to leave my current job to heal and rebuild myself as a man and a father. I resigned in May 2003 without another position lined up. I completely trusted God to provide." The circumstances of Scott's resignation were an unmistakable sign of how much he had changed. "When I resigned, I made it clear that I was willing to change my career and financial status in order to put my family first." Scott found another job that allowed more time with his family. He began exercising again and lost thirty-five pounds. And they started going back to church—as a family.

Cathy wanted to change, but, unlike Scott, she didn't have a drastic transformation right away. "I needed to heal and restore my relationship with the Lord first. I also had to figure out how to rebuild my broken spirit and how to keep it filled."

There was one particular song that she listened to over and over again that helped her. Its message was about choosing Christ over death. "Choosing Christ is what saved me on a daily basis," she remembers. "Even when I didn't want to be with Scott, I knew that choosing Christ meant choosing Scott." Cathy had completely fallen out of love with her husband—she didn't even like him. But she knew the right thing to do was to choose him. Then one day as she watched Scott play lovingly with the kids, she thought, for the first time in a long time, that he was handsome. The attraction was beginning to return.

"As the months progressed," Cathy explains, "we used many of the things we learned at the marriage intensive to build what we had always wanted but couldn't seem to find. We began to know each other better because we knew each other's heart. We no longer had secrets, and most importantly, we had Christ at the center of our relationship."

In January 2004, they renewed their vows in front of their friends. "God gave us a connection that we never thought possible.

For the first time we were unified as one team," Scott remembers. But by no means was it easy for the couple. "The first year was actually very difficult for me because of the memories," Scott admits. "Forgiveness of Cathy's sin was never once an issue. It was the forgetting that took time for me."

Their long talks have become a crucial part of their bonding. All subjects are now considered safe, and their openness with each other has opened new doors to increasing their love and trust. They finally see their marriage as a team effort.

Early in their marriage they didn't know how to fight, but they now interact on a regular basis to work out the conflicts that are a part of any relationship. "I don't avoid the issues anymore," Scott explains. "I engage with Cathy about things."

Cathy agrees. "It is so different when you are on the same team and realize that your spouse isn't your enemy. Only God could have restored the union between us, and now no one can separate us."

Forgiveness has also been key in rebuilding their bond. Scott describes how that works. "When people ask how I forgave Cathy so easily, I tell them that if Christ could die on the cross for our sins, how could I *not* forgive Cathy for her sin against me? Christ paid the price."

And for that, Scott is Cathy's hero. She feels rescued by his willingness to fight for her and change his ways. That's what she had wanted all along—to be protected and cherished by her husband. "It is putting God first and allowing Him to be our first love that makes all of this possible," Scott says. "I am now captivated by Cathy's beauty, and I feel more attracted to her now than the first time I laid eyes on her. What started out as physical attraction is now real, heart-binding admiration for who she is and for what God has done in her life. I am *so* blessed to have her as my wife."

Throughout their sixteen years of marriage, God has played a huge role in helping Scott and Cathy learn, grow, forgive, and love. He has surrounded them with supportive friends and mentors who have shown them what godly love looks like in an earthly context. Now, Scott and Cathy have become so passionate about helping other couples in crisis that they are making plans to enter marriage ministry full-time. They know that this type of career doesn't typically generate a lot of money, but they don't care and aren't worried. They are completely content and have peace in their marriage—and in their lives—at long last.

—As told to Jennifer Kabbany Dawson (with Julie Davis)

ᘓ • ᘓ

Scott and Cathy Jones found help for their troubled marriage through a marriage intensive held by the National Institute of Marriage (NIM). Founded by Smalley Ministries, NIM's goal is to provide "first response" resources to couples in crisis and to the churches that minister to them.

NIM's marriage intensives are often a life-changing experience for couples—or even solo spouses—who are struggling in their marriages. Monthly marriage conferences held in different parts of the country were developed as a result of the success of the counseling programs, while Marriage 911: First Response services were later added to assist church lay leaders in their initial response to couples in crisis.

National Institute of Marriage
250 Lakewood Drive
Hollister, MO 65671
(417) 335-5882
www.nationalmarriage.com
admin@nationalmarriage.com

I heard the words "I forgive you" roll off my tongue, as if this was a church play and I was a perfect little church mouse performing according to script. My mind could not grasp what was happening.

"Unbreak My Heart" by Toni Braxton blared from the car radio, and I sang along with gusto. *Perfect song. Right in my range*, I thought to myself as I sang with passion. *The words are completely depressing, though. Boy, that would be awful. Good thing I have a great marriage. I feel sorry for people who have to go through that kind of pain.*

I pulled into the garage that night and stepped into the house. I found Brian, my husband of nearly two decades, standing in the kitchen, his eyes filled with a strange sadness.

"Anne, we need to talk."

Over the past six months I had wondered whether Brian was depressed. Something was wrong inside of him. I had made every effort to find out what was wrong, but he had shut me out.

"I need to talk with you about something," Brian said again.

I waited. He looked into my eyes, then quickly looked away.

A slow fear began creeping up my body, starting at my feet.

"This is really difficult," Brian said. "I don't know how to say this. I don't know how to start. I really love you, Anne. I didn't mean for this to happen."

After what seemed like an eternity had passed, he continued.

"I'm involved with someone else."

•   •   •

I froze in place. An awkward silence elapsed. Then I heard the words "I forgive you" roll off my tongue, as if this was a church play and I was a perfect little church mouse performing according to script. My mind could not grasp what was happening. I felt as if I'd been shot, but somehow I was still breathing.

I sat down. I asked him some questions, and after a brief discussion I discovered my husband didn't even know whom he wanted to spend the rest of his life with. This other woman was already planning to divorce her own husband to marry mine. I went from great marriage to zero marriage in an instant. I didn't move from my chair all night. I just sat staring into the darkness in a state of shock. I needed someone to unbreak *my* heart now.

How could this have been happening to me? Why had there been no warning signs? If we had argued recently, maybe—but we had been getting along wonderfully. If sex had been less exciting—but we had been having great sex every night. Wasn't this kind of thing supposed to happen to people with problems in their marriages? It wasn't supposed to happen to strong couples like us!

During the days that followed, I walked around in a daze. I couldn't think straight. At times the pain became overwhelming. I went from feeling unbearable grief to raging anger to heroic vigilance.

Then a strange calm came over me, as if I no longer existed.

Three days passed before I could sleep. For twenty-five days I was unable to eat. Somehow I managed to perform the bare minimum of necessary tasks in order to care for my children. My love for them gave me the will to live.

"What about our wedding vows?" I asked Brian. "You promised

you were going to stay with me for a lifetime. You promised to be faithful to me—me and only me."

"That was then; this is now," he said.

That was it. My marriage had ended.

But a couple of days later, refusing to accept the end of my marriage, I wrote in my journal:

> *This is going to be the story of how our marriage went through death and was restored. I make this statement by faith at a time when it seems like it's over. But it ain't over 'til it's over. Today God laid restoration in my heart.*

I didn't understand what was happening, but I decided I wasn't going to let some woman waltz into my life and walk off with my husband just like that. I decided I was going to meet her.

My motive was simple: I wanted to see what she looked like. Her appearance could not remain a mystery to me for the rest of my life.

When I arrived, in place of the big-bosomed sex goddess I expected, I found a thin, average looking woman. On the outward beauty scale, Helen was clearly not my competition. *What did Brian see in her?*

I spoke to her with kindness, dignity, and grace. Nervously she opened up and told me her sad life story, unable to look me in the eyes. When it was my turn to talk, I replayed her life story back to her, explaining that marrying my husband was not going to solve the unhappiness in her life. She was speechless.

I left, feeling an unexplainable sensation of compassion for the woman who, only days earlier, I had fantasized about murdering. I felt like Superwoman because I met her misguided intentions with the power of love and truth. I faced my fear, and I wasn't afraid anymore.

BRIAN

During the affair a friend named Darrell reached out to me. After my first meeting with Darrell, I began to regain my senses and equilibrium concerning my affair with Helen. This was the first time I'd spoken about it with someone who didn't pass judgment on me, someone who actually listened to how I was feeling.

These conversations were a threat to Helen. She began to sense a loss of control in our situation. Helen wanted me to talk with her friends instead, since they would encourage me to leave my wife. Helen's insistence that I talk with her friends was the first sign I'd seen that she lacked concern for my happiness and well-being.

Darrell was the perfect person to talk to because he showed concern for me. He was neutral in the situation, and he himself was divorced because of an affair. Darrell's affair had cost him his marriage and his relationship with his kids. The affair, he said, hadn't been worth it. He listened instead of trying to tell me what to do. Best of all, he told me he would support me no matter what decision I made.

"But Brian," he said, "if you are planning to leave your wife and kids for another woman, you'd better make darn sure that she is way better looking, smarter, and nicer. She has to be richer and respect you more. And she needs to be way better in bed than what you have now, because if not, she isn't worth it!"

Of course Helen didn't meet any of these criteria. I told Darrell that I'd found Helen to be controlling and in a hurry to split up both of our marriages. I still had feelings for Helen, but the fairytale was starting to unravel.

ANNE

Two days later Brian walked into our house and said, "I guess I'm home," in a voice that gave the impression he didn't want to be.

What have I done? I thought. *Do I even want him back? Where are the flowers? Where is the part where he begs my forgiveness?*

I also discovered that he planned to remain "just friends" with the other woman!

Three weeks later, after careful deliberation, I wrote my husband an ultimatum letter. I promised that if he could commit to me exclusively, I would do everything within my power to be the most wonderful wife any man could ever have. I also told him in the letter, "If your friendship with Helen is so important to you, then there is no time like the present for you to leave. I won't make it difficult for you."

He crumpled the letter and threw it on the floor. I thought that was it. However, two days later, he ended his "friendship" with Helen.

●   ●   ●

Where the first three months post-disclosure had been a time of numbness and shock, the next three months were a time of intense fighting during which we began to deal with our issues. Even though our interactions were often intensely painful, there was also a strange sweetness. Through these honest disclosures we were becoming more fully known to each other. It is a powerful thing to be fully known and yet fully accepted.

Sometimes the pain got too intense. One day Brian was so overwhelmed with it that he picked up a six-pack of beer and drove along a winding canyon road. It was a hot, summer day, and one beer led to another. Somehow he went off the road and had an accident. Though he was uninjured, he totaled his vehicle and was picked up by police for drunk driving.

The following month, someone set our vehicle on fire in the middle of the night. An observant neighbor alerted us, and we ran outside. The vehicle was parked so close to the house that the fire had begun to burn the garage door; it could have burned down the whole house—with us inside. Thanks to that neighbor, we were able to douse the fire before significant damage was done to our home.

Police informed us that the fire was not a random act. "Who's mad at you?" they wanted to know. Brian confessed he'd had an affair and the other woman's husband wasn't happy. After a police investigation, no one was found guilty, but it was clear that someone intended us harm.

The next month we found ourselves in the hospital with our beloved teenage daughter. In a desperate attempt to get our attention, she had overdosed on pills and nearly died. It wasn't enough to almost lose my husband; now I'd almost lost one of my children as well.

It was a nightmare. I was going from crisis to crisis, feeling sure each time that my life could not possibly get any worse, only to encounter a new disaster around every corner. I often wondered if it was sane to believe I would ever know a single day of happiness again.

Brian

I was determined to do whatever it took to win back Anne's love and respect. She was worth it. I believed we could overcome this terrible deed I had committed. I wasn't unrealistic, though. From the very beginning, I knew it would take a lot of time and effort and that Anne would not "just get over it."

It was so hard to look into the eyes of the woman I truly loved and see the pain I'd caused. It wasn't easy to revisit the "why" questions, yet discussion was the only way for her to get the answers she needed. My openness helped her to regain trust in me. Many times, though, it felt like we were not making any progress.

I was reading books that were helping me to understand myself and how I could have done something that I was morally and intellectually opposed to. This helped me to avoid defensiveness about my actions when Anne asked questions that made me look bad or selfish. I needed to recognize my own weaknesses and overcome them to ensure I would never have another affair.

I was trying to treat Anne like a princess. I wanted to make it up to her for what I had done. I wanted to show Anne that I really, really loved her and was willing to prove it to her by my words and my actions.

Yet no matter how much we talked, how many times I answered her questions, how many coffees we shared, or how much money I spent on her, it felt like we were not moving forward. But I wasn't prepared to give up, because I loved her.

So I wrote a letter to her explaining how I could not bear the thought that the person I love could not respect me.

Anne

I did respect him. I didn't understand why I was falling hopelessly short of communicating that love and respect to him. I apologized for not listening. As we talked, I felt a little more hopeful about our future, until Brian shared something a friend had said to him that day.

"Considering the way you were feeling," this friend had told Brian, "it's surprising you didn't have an affair years earlier."

I was furious. How dare someone say I deserved for this to happen to me? How dare someone insinuate that it was inevitable? Did this person not have a clue how painful affairs are to the one who is betrayed?

I demanded to know who it was, but Brian wouldn't tell me.

"Anne, I *have* felt disrespected and not listened to by you for some time," he said. "I've tried to tell you this many times over the years, but you would never listen to me. You became defensive and told me I was wrong for feeling that way. Then you would get depressed for days and start saying that I didn't love you, and then I would have to spend what felt like forever proving my love to you."

As I heard Brian say this, I felt as though I had been living inside a bubble, in a fairytale world believing only what I had wanted to believe. Now my bubble was being burst. I could no longer remain in the idealism I longed for. I was doing everything within my psyche to keep that painful truth and reality out. I didn't want to see my own fault in the relationship breakdown. It hurt too much.

Finally Brian confessed that it was one of our closest friends who had said this, a man I *knew* genuinely cared about us. I called the man the next morning for an explanation.

"I'm not saying that you deserved for this to happen to you," he explained kindly. "I'm saying that considering the way Brian has been feeling on the inside, it's surprising he didn't have an affair sooner. The man has been so frustrated. You do not communicate your respect toward him."

He explained how I was always expecting perfection from Brian, how I really wasn't overlooking his faults, and how I didn't listen but spent all my time correcting his speech instead of hearing what he had to say.

For the first time I saw how even though I was a good wife and had the best of intentions, I had unknowingly caused pain in my husband's life, much the same as my husband had caused me pain.

I was finally able to see my part in the relationship breakdown. I opened my heart to the truth and allowed the false security of my fairytale bubble to fade away, replacing it with reality. What was reality? I was not a perfect wife, Brian was not a perfect husband, and we did not have a perfect marriage. But in the midst of all of our imperfections, our love for one another was very real.

This was a major turning point in the healing of our relationship, and I don't believe we could ever have healed if I hadn't reached it. After a big cry, I wrote a letter to my husband apologizing for not understanding his needs, for not listening or respecting him, for playing the role of the "noble one" in the relationship, and for making him out to be the one who didn't quite measure up.

I wrote that letter six months after the day I learned of Brian's affair. I doubt I would have been able to write it a day sooner.

BRIAN

After receiving that letter, I felt relief and hope for our future for the first time. Through everything, even the affair, I loved Anne deeply, but I had been unable to communicate my needs to her. At last Anne had been able to really hear me, to hear the truth of my side, how I was feeling. For the first time I felt understood.

Seven years have passed since this time of darkness in our lives. Today we're happier and more in love than either of us imagined possible. One of our greatest rewards has been earning the respect of our children. They told us, "Most of our friends' parents have had the exact same problems as you and Dad have had, except most of them just quit and got divorced. You and Dad worked out your problems. We really respect you for that." Coming from teenagers, this was profound.

ANNE

As sad as the affair was, I would not want to go back to what I call my "pre-affair" existence. Many times I have thought to myself, *If only I could have gotten here some other way. Why did I have to go through so much pain?* But I really don't know what else would have gotten my attention.

No matter what tragedies happen in our lives, we always have a choice—not a choice over what will happen to us, but a choice over how we will react to it. Will we become bitter or better? I chose to become better, and now my greatest tragedy has also become my greatest personal victory.

Today, I can truly say that my husband's affair became the best thing that ever happened to me!

— Anne and Brian Bercht

⊂⊃ • ⊂⊃

Anne Bercht is the author of the book *My Husband's Affair Became the Best Thing That Ever Happened to Me*. She and her husband, Brian, also run the Beyond Affairs Network (BAN) and host Passionate Life Seminars.

BAN is made up of local support groups that provide help and healing for men and women recovering from the heartbreak of a spouse's affair, enabling them to proactively move forward and recover. Passionate Life Seminars are an investment in marriage, even for those who have never had to deal with infidelity. Four unique seminars are offered: "The Passionate Marriage Evening", "Embracing Our Differences", "Healing from Affairs", and "Love and Passion: Reigniting the Flame." Personal marriage coaching is also available.

Passionate Life Seminars and
The Beyond Affairs Network
P. O. Box 1562
Sumas, WA 98295-1562

(604) 859-9393
www.passionatelife.ca
www.beyondaffairs.com
info@beyondaffairs.com

Vandana wanted to stay home with her baby, but they simply couldn't afford it. They had no budget, no savings, no investments, no plan, and no idea how to make one.

"Get out!"

Vandana's father was enraged. He practically forced David out the door. "Get out, and don't ever come near my daughter again!"

What a disaster that had been.

When he and Vandana had made the decision to finally tell her parents about their engagement, they'd known the meeting would be tense. But this was worse than either of them had imagined. Now, with Vandana's father angrily blocking his reentry to the house, David had no choice but to get in his truck and drive home.

The couple had kept their relationship a secret for nearly two years. They'd been engaged for one of those years. Neither of them had wanted to keep the secret from her family, but they felt they had no choice. Growing up in a traditional Indian family, Vandana wasn't even allowed to have non-Indian friends, let alone date a white American man.

Tradition determined that when Vandana came of age, she would enter into an arranged marriage with an Indian man of her own caste. Vandana had resigned herself to this reality and had never considered another option — until she met David in her college algebra class. He was a determined, rough-necked Southern boy who wouldn't take no for an answer.

DAVID'S DREAM GIRL

When David saw Vandana walk into class that first day, he literally fell out of his chair. For years, he'd had dreams of meeting a petite, brown-eyed, dark-skinned beauty. Vandana was his dream girl in the flesh. It took him a few days to gather the courage to sit next to her, and he racked his brain for an excuse to talk to her.

Finally, he devised a plan. One day in class he casually introduced himself to Vandana and told her that the campus bookstore had run out of algebra textbooks (which was true). He asked if he could make copies of their assignments from her book. She obliged, and thus began multiple walks to the library for copy making.

David was smart. His plan allowed them to get to know each other in a no-pressure environment. He wanted Vandana to feel comfortable around him before he asked her out. His strategy was working. Soon, the bookstore restocked, and their library walks came to an end. But their future was just beginning.

One day David gathered the courage to ask Vandana to the state fair. He was shocked and a little hurt when she flatly responded, "I can't." She hadn't told him about her family situation. A few days later he asked her out again, and again she replied, "I can't." This time he pressed her to tell him why.

Embarrassed, Vandana finally admitted that she wasn't allowed to go on dates. But she said she liked him and wanted to spend time with him. Eventually they arrived at a solution: lunch dates. Her parents would never have to know. Each day they looked forward to their time together at the park.

The next semester they arranged their class schedules so that they could spend all afternoon together. Their lunch meetings went on for months. The months stretched into a year, and before long they were engaged. All the while, Vandana's parents knew nothing of the relationship.

Until that night.

BREAKING WITH TRADITION

While her father was forcibly escorting David from the house, Vandana was in the living room surrounded by her mother and siblings, who were all furious with her. They saw Vandana's behavior as a direct assault to their family. She had disrespected their traditions, culture, and way of life. Crushed, Vandana excused herself from the madness, shut herself in her room, and cried herself to sleep.

In the days following her confession of love for "the American," Vandana's home situation grew frighteningly volatile. David quickly prepared a room for her at the duplex he shared with his mother. Vandana left home, and for three days her family had no idea where she was. Finally she called her sister to tell her that she was safe.

She agreed to come home if her family would just calm down. She and David were engaged, and there was nothing her parents could do to change that. If they couldn't accept that fact, she wasn't coming back. Her parents begrudgingly obliged, figuring that this was a phase Vandana would eventually grow out of.

But they didn't make things easy for the young couple. They forbade David from calling Vandana at home or entering their house. And when she transferred to a larger college to complete her accounting degree, they offered no financial support whatsoever.

David took on the responsibility of supporting himself and his fiancée. He worked full-time and took night classes to continue his own education. Most of Vandana's tuition was covered by her work-study scholarship, but David paid the rest of her bills and made sure she always had gas in her car. He wanted her to be able to focus on getting through school since they had decided not to marry until she graduated.

Those few years were difficult. But even so, their love grew. After four years of dating, David and Vandana finally married. They exchanged vows just one month after Vandana's college graduation. Finally they could enjoy being together, no more obstacles.

TOGETHER AT LAST

Life was wonderful for a time. They coasted along blissfully, just happy to be together. Nothing could keep them apart. They each worked full-time jobs, but they still made time to go out, have fun, and socialize. Vandana was thrilled to finally be able to experience all the things she'd been restricted from throughout her childhood.

After the wedding, Vandana's parents gradually grew to accept David. They eventually welcomed him as part of the family. David and Vandana were happier than they had ever been.

But in all marriages the honeymoon eventually fades and reality sets in.

Soon the newness wore off, leaving two very different personalities from two very different backgrounds trying to "make it work." Financial issues were particularly stressful for the young couple. As hard as they worked, they couldn't seem to get ahead financially. The more money they made, the more they spent.

The situation worsened after their first child, Megan, was born. Vandana wanted to stay home with her baby, but they simply couldn't afford it. Now they had a mortgage, a car loan, and ever-increasing credit card debt. They had no budget, no savings, no investments, no plan, and no idea how to make one.

IF WE COULD JUST MAKE MORE MONEY . . .

The couple thought their financial struggles would be solved if David went back to school. With his transportation and logistics degree in hand, they felt he could land a better-paying job. He enrolled in school full-time and took on a part-time job as well. By the time David graduated, Vandana was pregnant with their son, Max. With a new baby on the way, David was even more determined to provide for his growing family.

David was able to find a much better job. But their financial situation did not improve. Their increased income just gave them a higher ceiling to jump to. David and Vandana felt a great deal of pressure to keep up with the Joneses, leading to the acquisition of more and more things. They were making more money than ever, but they had no financial freedom. They had become slaves to their lifestyle.

At one point, both David and Vandana came down with the flu at the same time. They panicked, realizing that at the rate they were spending, neither of them could afford to miss a single day of work. Something had to change.

On the radio they had heard about a financial seminar by a man named Dave Ramsey. They volunteered to work the event so they could take the classes for free. After the seminar, the couple talked about what they had learned, but they failed to make any lifestyle changes as a result. Soon the words of the speaker faded, and they were back to where they had started.

CULTURE CLASH

The couple's problems were more than just financial. The differences in their cultural backgrounds and upbringings manifested more and more as they became parents. Vandana had been raised

Hindu, but she had always found the stories and rituals surrounding the religion to be confusing and had never felt a personal connection with any of the gods she had learned about as a child. Religion had never been an important part of her life or her marriage.

But when Megan was born, something changed. She began to worry constantly. She worried that something would happen to her daughter or to her or David. She began to wonder about eternal things and the purpose of her life. She found no comfort or answers in the religion of her childhood, so she began to look elsewhere for something to ease her anxiety and answer her questions.

Before long, a friend invited her to church, and soon Vandana was helping out at a weekly children's Bible club. She was fascinated by the thought of a God who loved her and wanted to know her personally. This God was so different from the Hindu gods that had always seemed cold, distant, and impersonal.

David was less than thrilled by Vandana's involvement in church. He had been raised Southern Baptist but had stopped going as a teenager when his grandfather had died of cancer. David's grandfather had been there for him when his own unstable father hadn't been. So when his grandfather died, David blamed God. Now, as a grown man, David had completely ruled religion out of his life. He had spent years cursing the God he tried so hard not to believe in. Vandana's interest in Christianity awoke volatile feelings in David and increased the conflict between them.

The stress caused by the couple's job situations only served to worsen their marriage relationship. David was miserable, working seventy hours a week as a supervisor in a shop where union battles created a perpetually hostile and unpredictable environment. But he felt trapped. He couldn't afford to work fewer hours or quit or even take time off to look for another job. His family depended on every penny of his paycheck. Soon, David found himself disconnecting from his family and sinking into a dark depression.

Vandana wasn't happy with her job as a CPA. She was over-worked and didn't get along with her boss. As her family grew, so did her desire to stay home with her children, but they still couldn't afford for her to. As time went on, she grew disillusioned with her life. She was consumed by an unsatisfying job, overwhelming financial stress, and a home life that demanded more than she could give. She began to slip into depression as well.

Then came her breaking point.

A SEARCH FOR PURPOSE

On the way to a doctor's appointment one day, Vandana suddenly had the urge to turn the car around and drive to the church where she had been volunteering. She realized she needed to talk to a pastor as soon as possible.

As she drove, scenes from her life began replaying in her mind. She wondered how all the events and circumstances of her life had led her to this state of desperation. She knew from listening to the stories at the Bible club that the Christian God offered hope in dark situations and that He could also make good things come out of a painful past. She knew He could give purpose to a life that seemingly had none. She wanted hope and purpose. She needed it.

She ran breathlessly into the pastor's office and asked him to pray with her.

The pastor talked with her, read some key Scripture verses, and prayed with her. Vandana walked out of his office with a new pair of eyes. She began to see everything in a completely different light. She all but floated home and tried to explain to David what had happened to her.

David wasn't sure what to think at first. While he was glad his wife seemed to have gotten some peace, he also feared she was being brainwashed by the church she was attending. It certainly didn't ease his concern when, in the following days, Vandana proceeded to have a nervous breakdown, missing more than a month of work as a result. David blamed this on the church and her recent "conversion." She had seemed fine before. But now religion was messing up his wife and threatening his own sanity.

What David didn't realize was that Vandana had not been fine for a very long time.

For years she had buried her anger, confusion, and childhood pain under a guise of self-sufficiency. But when she made the decision to put her life in God's hands, she realized she couldn't keep everything buried anymore. A lifetime's worth of pent-up emotion spilled out of her. The intensity of it all left Vandana incapacitated for a while. The difference was that she recognized it as the beginning of a healing process that had needed to happen for a long time. She sought counseling and began to get a healthy perspective on her life.

But David didn't see the real reasons behind his wife's meltdown. He just thought his wife had gone crazy and it was the church's fault. He began objecting heavily to her attending church, and he especially didn't want her to take the children. He didn't want to risk them being brainwashed like their mother.

Soon, David and Vandana were fighting all the time. If it wasn't about religion, it was about finances. Vandana desperately wanted some financial security. As a CPA, she became very familiar with other people's financial strategies and saw that it was indeed possible to reach a place of financial health. She began to talk to David about what she was learning at work. She finally saw the importance of budgeting, saving, investing, and planning. But David wasn't interested in making those kinds of changes. His solution was to take out a second mortgage on the house.

STALEMATE

As the couple drifted further apart, David spent much of his time and energy at work, while continuing to battle clinical depression. He went to counseling and took his medication, but he still wasn't pleasant to be around. Vandana wasn't very easy to get along with at this point, either. She had become resentful toward David and stopped being attentive to him as a husband or even a person. She focused her efforts on reaching her goal of financial stability and on being the best mother she could be. She made sure her children were involved in lots of extracurricular activities. She was determined that they would have all the opportunities she had not had as a child.

Neither David nor Vandana put any effort into improving their relationship. They even separated briefly at one point, but they soon fell back into their tumultuous coexistence. After a few years of stalemate, Vandana couldn't take any more. She filed for divorce.

David moved in with his mother while Vandana continued living at their home with the children. She started her own CPA firm from home and worked frantically to build her financial independence.

As the divorce proceedings continued, David hit an all-time low. He was still miserable at work, he was sinking in debt, and it seemed as if he had lost his family for good. His only source of comfort was his mother. She and David had long talks about her own struggles earlier in her life and how her faith in God had helped her through them. David usually shut down whenever someone started talking to him about God or faith, but now he was just desperate enough to listen. Her gentle words gradually began to soften his heart.

A DIVINE TWO-BY-FOUR

Early one morning before sunrise, he sat on the steps outside his mother's house, restless and unable to sleep. Inexplicably, he began to feel emotions he had never felt before. In his mind's eye, he began to see the faces of his wife and children and physically feel the pain they had experienced through his words and actions over the years. He began to clearly see the mistakes he had made and how they had impacted situations and people in his life. He couldn't believe he had been so blind for so long.

Trembling, he ran inside the house and woke his mother, frantically asking her to pray with him.

David says that was the morning God took a two-by-four to his head. He developed an insatiable desire to learn about God and to know truth. He was beginning to understand the life change Vandana had experienced, and he was eager to share his newfound faith with her. With the divorce looming on the horizon, he asked her to attend a church service with him on the Fourth of July. She agreed.

After the service, a man spontaneously asked them out to lunch. David and this man became good friends, and they began reading and studying the Bible together regularly. In his personal prayer time, David realized he had built a wall around his heart as a teenager, and his fear and pride kept anyone from getting close to him. The only person he had truly let in was Vandana, but now he had managed to push her away as well.

With the divorce all but final, David went to his wife and, on the front porch of the home they used to share, apologized. He admitted he had been prideful and stubborn, and he asked her to forgive him. He assured her that he had made the decision to follow Christ regardless of the outcome of their marriage.

Vandana couldn't deny he had changed, but she was skeptical.

Still unsure of how to respond to David, she talked to a marriage counselor. The woman encouraged Vandana to extend grace to her husband. Unconvinced, Vandana asked her, "What if it's not real?" The counselor responded, "What if it is?"

WORTH THE RISK

Vandana decided to take the chance. They called off the divorce, and David moved back home. This time they were both committed to making the needed changes in their relationship.

They addressed their financial crisis by attending more of Dave Ramsey's Financial Peace seminars and actually applying the principles to their lives. They began living on a budget, which enabled them to start paying off their debt, and they started putting money into savings. They decided to track the results of these changes to make sure they were staying on target. Eventually they began setting long-term goals and asking God for wisdom as they made five- and ten-year plans for their family. Vandana finally had the financial security she had so longed for.

Spiritually, they grew as a couple and as a family. He and Vandana committed themselves to praying and reading the Bible together and individually. In doing so, David learned how to humbly lead his family, and Vandana learned how to love and respect her husband. David quit his job and began working from home with Vandana. This enabled him to spend more time with his wife and children. David became a Cub Scout leader and a soccer coach for his daughter's team. He even joined the church choir.

As they continued to grow and learn, they felt compelled to become Financial Peace seminar facilitators. David and Vandana wanted to help other couples who were going through situations similar to theirs. With all they had gone through, they knew they had a lot to offer.

Recently, David and Vandana moved into a beautiful four-bedroom house, more than twice the size of their previous home. Even though they aren't making as much money as they once were, they have learned to manage the money they make. They worked their way out of debt just three years after setting their financial goals. And they now have plenty of savings, an emergency fund, and money for retirement. They still have a house payment, but it's manageable, and everything else they own is paid for.

David and Vandana are living in a financial freedom they never could have imagined before. And since they've both dedicated their lives to God and to each other, they're happier and more fulfilled than they ever thought possible. More than the financial freedom David and Vandana have achieved, they value the spiritual freedom they have in Christ.

David still marvels at how that dark-eyed beauty from his childhood dreams became his lover, his best friend, and his traveling partner on an unexpected journey to faith, healing, and the discovery of God's ultimate purpose for both of their lives.

—As told to Erika Chambers

⌒•⌒

David and Vandana found financial help for their marriage through Dave Ramsey's program, Financial Peace University.

Financial disagreements are one of the top causes of divorce. Financial Peace University is a class designed to cover topics including saving money, communicating about finances, planning for the future, debt elimination in as little as 13 weeks, and the joy of giving. A variety of other courses are also available, from church programs to teen studies. Currently, over 500,000 families have experienced the positive effects of skills learned in the Financial Peace University class.

Financial Peace University
Dave Ramsey
www.daveramsey.com

"WHY ME?" *or* "WHAT NOW?"

A Call to Action by Dr. Leo Godzich,
Founder and President of NAME
(National Association of Marriage Enhancement)

When we are faced with the heartache of a challenging or seemingly impossible marital circumstance, we often cry out, "Why me?"

I'd like to respectfully challenge you to resist asking yourself that question.

Adam and Eve were forbidden by God to eat of the tree of the knowledge of good and evil—in essence, the tree of *why?* In launching more than two hundred biblical counseling centers in ten countries and training multitudes of counselors, I frequently remind people that the human desire to fully know *why* is vanity. It places our "right" to understand as greater than God's ability to do what He chooses.

Our challenge is not to ask "Why me?" but to ask "What now?"

Whenever I see a seemingly hopeless marriage restored, I remind the couple that how they view their relationship now is far different than what their perspective was when they were going through their crisis.

The "What now?" question is proactive. It moves us toward progress, even when we lack understanding of what is going on at the moment.

So now you have read all the inspiring stories in this book. Perhaps you are not sure how they apply to you or whether there is someone who could help you understand what you should do now. The organizations listed at the end of each chapter have been carefully selected because of their ability and willingness to help people just like you. They are indeed heralds of hope who will help you figure out the answers to the question "What now?"

Most marriage and family therapists today are told in their training that by the time a couple comes to see them, it is usually too late to help. But don't you believe that. As absurd as it seems, many therapists are trained to help couples go their separate ways amicably rather than move people toward true restoration.

All of the organizations in this book have been chosen because they believe otherwise. Their mission is to help you obtain the skills, tools, and motivation to move your marriage toward reconciliation and restoration.

Each story in this book is unique—just like your marriage. Choose one of the organizations found in this book and contact them, believing with more hope than you had when you started reading this book that the answer is on the way.

If you want our help directly, contact NAME at info@name-online.net or toll-free at (888) 262-NAME (6263).

Finally, if you have a restored marriage or if you have read this book because you rejoice for restored marriages, send the publisher your story. Who knows? It may appear in the next edition. Your story might just help save another marriage.

ALL *is* RIGHT

*A song by Erika Chambers—a child who watched her parents
fall in love again.*

Last night I saw you kiss her on the porch
I watched you from the window
Just before I turned my covers down
Now I can go to sleep and know
That everything is right
With the world, with the night
All is right.

I listen to you laugh outside my room
You're whispering your nothings,
And you don't think I can hear you
But when I go to sleep I know
That everything is right
With the world, with the night
All is right.

And I can rest my head upon
The thought of you still going strong
And I can dream of days I know will be
When a love like yours will find me

Tonight I watched you dancing in the dark
To music from a stereo you set beneath the stars
Now I can go to sleep and know
That everything is right
With the world, with the night
All is right.

All is right

RECOMMENDED MARRIAGE RESOURCES

The following organizations offer a variety of resources designed to heal and strengthen marriages.

MARRIAGE CRISIS HELP FOR MULTIPLE ISSUES

Divorce Busting
Michele Weiner-Davis
Boulder, CO
(800) 664-2435
www.divorcebusting.com
michele@divorcebusting.com

Family Dynamics Institute
Franklin, TN
(800) 650-9995
www.familydynamics.net

Family Foundations International
Craig and Jan Hill
Littleton, CO
(303) 797-1139
www.familyfoundations.com
info@familyfi.org

The International Center for
    Reconciling God's Way
Joe and Michelle Williams
(800) 205-6808
www.reconcilinggodsway.org
reconcile@reconcilinggodsway.org

Inverse Ministries, Inc.
Clint and Penny Bragg
Port Orange, FL
www.inverseministries.org
reconcile@inverseministries.org

Life Partners Christian Ministries
Ken and Nancy Nair
Phoenix, AZ
(602) 485-5115
www.lifepartners.org
ken@lifepartners.org

Retrouvaille
(800) 470-2230
www.retrouvaille.org

National Institute of Marriage
Hollister, MO
(417) 335-5882
www.nationalmarriage.com
admin@nationalmarriage.com

Restoration Resources Ministry, Inc.
Pastor Tim and Linda Buttrey
Beavercreek, OH
(937) 510-5595
www.restorationresources.us
tim@restorationresources.us

aved Marriage Network
Hendersonville, TN
www.savedmarriagenetwork.com

The Third Option
Syracuse, NY
(315) 472-6728
www.thethirdoption.com
pat@thethirdoption.com

Troubled With
(A Ministry of Focus on the Family)
(800) A-Family
www.troubledwith.com

MARRIAGE CRISIS HELP FOR SPECIFIC ISSUES

Adultery
Beyond Affairs Network
Passionate Life Seminars
Anne and Brian Bercht
Sumas, WA
(604) 859-9393
www.beyondaffairs.com
info@beyondaffairs.com

Bob and Audrey Meisner
www.bobandaudrey.com
Audrey@bobandaudrey.com
Bob@bobandaudrey.com

Hope & Healing Ministries, Inc.
Gary and Mona Shriver
Denair, CA
(209) 667-5012
www.hopeandhealing.us
info@hopeandhealing.us

Nancy C. Anderson
Huntington Beach, CA
(714) 206-9540
www.nancycanderson.com
ncawrites@msn.com

Baggage From the Past
The Institute for Soul Healing Love
Drs. Beverly and Tom Rodgers
Charlotte, NC
(704) 364-9176
www.soulhealinglove.com
info@soulhealinglove.com

Emotional/Mental Instability
Amen Clinics
Newport Beach, CA
(888) 564-2700
www.amenclinics.com

Pine Rest Christian Mental Health Services
Grand Rapids, MI
(616) 455-5000
www.pinerest.org

Financial Crisis
Financial Peace University
(A ministry of Dave Ramsey)
Brentwood, TN
www.daveramsey.com

Crown Financial Ministries
Gainesville, GA
(800) 722-1976
www.crown.org

Help for Couples in Ministry
Encouragement Dynamics
Dr. Gary Pinion
Richland, WA
(509) 521-5014
www.encouragementdynamics.com
gpinion@aol.com

Shepherd's Heart Ministries
Larry and Lorrie Russell
Parker, CO
(303) 884-8030
www.shepherdsheartministry.com
shepherdshrt@aol.com

MARRIAGE RESOURCES 253

Loss of a Child

Healing Hearts Ministries
Bonney Lake, WA
(360) 897-2711
www.healinghearts.org

Smile Again Ministries
Sauk Rapids, MN
(320) 310-8877
www.smileagainministries.com

Sexual Addiction

Be Broken Ministries, Inc.
Jonathan Daugherty
San Antonio, TX
(800) 49-PURITY
www.bebroken.com
www.puresexradio.com
jonathan@bebroken.com

Bethesda Workshops
Marnie C. Ferree
Nashville, TN 37204
(866) 464-HEAL
www.bethesdaworkshops.org
nhobson@bethesdaworkshops.org

Faithful and True Ministries
Eden Prairie, MN
(952) 746-3882
www.faithfulandtrueministries.com
mlaaser@aol.com

Healing for the Soul
Colorado Springs, CO
(719) 590-SOUL
www.healingforthesoul.org
info@healingforthesoul.org

LIFE (Living in Freedom Everyday)
  Ministries
(866) 408-LIFE
www.freedomeveryday.org

Standing for Your Marriage Alone

Covenant Keepers (U.S.)
Tulsa, OK
(918) 743-0365
www.covenantkeepersinc.org
info@covenantkeepersinc.org
Rejoice Marriage Ministries
Pompano Beach, FL 33061
www.rejoiceministries.org

Stepfamily Issues

Instep Ministries
Jeff and Judi Parziale
Tucson, AZ
(520) 721-0800
www.instepministries.com
info@instepministries.com

Successful Stepfamilies
Ron Deal
Amarillo, TX
(806) 356-7701
www.successfulstepfamilies.com
nan.deal@successfulstepfamilies.com

MARRIAGE STRENGTHENING ORGANIZATIONS

Family Life
Little Rock, AR
(800) FL-TODAY
www.familylife.com

Fortified Marriages
Chris and Carmen Garner
Chandler, AZ
(866) 263-5638
www.fortifiedmarriages.com
info@fortifiedmarriages.com

Marriage Savers of Frederick County
Rev. Robert J. Donk
Walkersville, MD
(301) 898-8917
www.marriagesaversfrederick.org
bob@marriagesaversfrederick.org

Marriage Savers, Inc.
   (National Office)
Mike and Harriet McManus
Potomac, MD
(301) 469-5873
www.marriagesavers.org

NAME (National Association of
   Marriage Enhancement)
Phoenix, AZ
(888) 262-NAME
www.nameonline.net
info@nameonline.net

Radical Love (Center on Christian
   Relationships)
Buford, GA
(770) 945-8962
www.radicallove.org

Two Equal One
Lakewood, CO
(303) 933-3331
www.2equal1.com

**Contact these organizations to
find out how you can bring effective marriage ministry to your
community.**

AMFM (Association of Marriage
   and Family Ministries)
Eric and Jennifer Garcia, Cofounders
Scottsdale, AZ
(480) 718-3020
www.amfmonline.com
staff@amfmonline.com

NAME (National Association of
   Marriage Enhancement)
Dr. Leo and Molly Godzich,
   Cofounders and Directors
Phoenix, AZ
(888) 262-NAME
www.nameonline.net
info@nameonline.net

Saved Marriage Network
Mae Chambers, Founder and
   President
Hendersonville, TN
www.savedmarriagenetwork.com

Smart Marriages
The Coalition for Marriage, Family,
   and Couples Education
Diane Sollee, Founder and Director
Washington DC
(202) 362-3332
www.smartmarriages.com
cmfce@smartmarriages.com

TOPICAL INDEX

While many of the following issues are found in several of our stories in some capacity, this index only notates the page numbers of the stories in which the related issue is a central theme.

ACKNOWLEDGMENTS

First and foremost, we thank God. Without Him there is no hope. Thanks to John, Adam, Aly, and Terry—our wonderfully supportive family who graciously put up with more than a year of our tunnel vision and eager ramblings. To every couple whose story is told in this book, thank you for your willingness to share your miracle with the world. To all the ministries involved in this project, thank you for believing in us, encouraging us, and praying for us. We pray that countless hurting couples will find help through your ministry as a result of this book. Thanks to Lisa, Jennifer, Heather, Eric, Patrick, and Chelsea for lending your talent and creativity to bring these stories to life. Thanks to Jeff for holding our green little hands, to Debbie for your rapt attention to detail, and to Pat for your exquisite interior design. Thanks to Kirk for finding the perfect sunset, to Steve for your brilliance and brutal honesty, and to Devin for giving up that weekend for our sake. Thank you, Pastor Leo Godzich (NAME), Phil Waugh (The Covenant Marriage Movement), Eric and Jennifer Garcia (AMFM), and Diane Solee (Smart Marriages). Your passion is inspiring. To the staff of PlastiCard+Plus, thanks for sharing your boss with a book. Thank you, Beth, Pam, Sarah, and Annie, for super-proofing. Thank you, Joyce Hart, for sharing your wisdom. To Pam and Bobby, thank you for your fervent prayers for us and for this project. And to Dwain Chambers and Dick Sleeper, thank you for continually bugging Mae to write this book. It took ten years or so, but here it is. Finally.

And thank you to Pastor Maury Davis for challenging our thinking concerning crisis marriage ministry and the Church.

Most sincerely,
Mae and Erika Chambers